An award-winning journalist, Shaili Chopra has written four books and is the founder of India's biggest platform for women-centric stories, SheThePeople.TV, which reaches over 15 million viewers through its online and offline network. It has documented more than 50,000 stories of women, each fearless and fierce. Chopra received the Vital Voices Fellowship (established by Hillary Clinton and Madeleine Albright). She was named Woman Entrepreneur of the Year Award by Entrepreneur.com, and was announced as one of India's Top 50 Most Influential Women in Media by Impact. She has spoken at various TEDx events, and moderated at World Economic Forum initiatives. She believes women should take a chance on themselves and break the glass ceiling in every single sphere of life. Her non-fiction books have been published to critical acclaim.

Meghna Pant is an award-winning author, journalist, feminist and speaker. Her books have been published to critical and commercial acclaim. Pant's debut collection of short stories, *Happy Birthday* (2013), was longlisted for the Frank O'Connor International Award (2014), the world's most prestigious short-story prize. *One & a Half Wife* (2012)—her bestselling debut novel—won the national Muse India Young Writer Award and was shortlisted for several other awards, including the Amazon Breakthrough Novel Award. *The Trouble with Women* (2016) is considered a landmark in feminist writing and was described as 'the best book from Juggernaut' by the *Hindu BusinessLine*. Pant has also won the FON South Asia Short Story Award (2016) and the Bharat Nirman Award (2017) for her writing. Her short story *Cows That Glow* was longlisted for the Commonwealth Short Story Prize (2018).

Feminist Rani

India's Most Powerful Voices
on Gender Equality

SHAILI CHOPRA
MEGHNA PANT

PENGUIN BOOKS

An imprint of Penguin Random House

PENGUIN BOOKS

USA | Canada | UK | Ireland | Australia
New Zealand | India | South Africa | China

Penguin Books is part of the Penguin Random House group of companies
whose addresses can be found at global.penguinrandomhouse.com

Published by Penguin Random House India Pvt. Ltd
7th Floor, Infinity Tower C, DLF Cyber City,
Gurgaon 122 002, Haryana, India

First published in Penguin Books by Penguin Random House India 2018

ISBN 9780143442875

Typeset in Bembo Std by Manipal Digital Systems, Manipal
Printed at Thomson Press India Ltd, New Delhi

www.penguin.co.in

Contents

Prologue   vii

Introduction   xiii

Kalki Koechlin   1

Gurmehar Kaur   15

Sapna Bhavnani   27

Aditi Mittal   37

Tanmay Bhat   49

Deepa Malik   59

Malishka Mendonsa   75

Gul Panag   87

Ankhi Das   109

Aarefa Johari   123

Rohini Shirke   139

Rana Ayyub   153

Sorabh Pant   173

Shree Gauri Sawant   181

Prologue

In 2013, when I began lending my voice to the feminist movement, people thought I was crazy. At that time, not many had come out as feminists. Feminism was considered a bad word. Feminists were pigeonholed into women who were angry and aggressive. The movement was associated with male-bashing. In fact, some feminists would not admit to being feminists because their husbands or boyfriends or fathers or brothers would disapprove! Even within feminism, women felt compelled to define their needs in terms of what men wanted.

Due to these misrepresentations, some people claimed I was too 'normal' to be a feminist. Although I was righteously angry, and assertive, I was neither an angry nor an aggressive person. I didn't hate men. I wanted to get married and have children. The horror! A couple of people were also of the fine opinion that I didn't 'look' like a feminist because I had long hair, wore pencil skirts, and occasionally put on lipstick. They wanted me to pander to certain stereotypes, while I was trying to break them! Obviously, I wasn't having any of it, because being who you are *doesn't* make you any less of a feminist. Feminism is not about being a 'type'.

It's about exercising your own choice of representation, discourse and agency.

Fast-forward to 2018. Thanks in part to the #MeToo movement, the amplification of personal narratives, women's marches, collective outrage, increasing awareness, and social media, misogyny has been given a flip-off. Being a feminist is suddenly 'cool'. It's become a part of the popular lexicon in India. Young people wear 'I Am A Feminist' T-shirts. Women and men own it, including celebrities such as Kangana Ranaut, Farhan Akhtar, Priyanka Chopra and Vidya Balan. Even non-celebrity feminists are considered role models. After centuries of protests and formations, feminism has finally become palatable to the masses.

Despite this, and the many opportunities and liberties that we owe to the feminist movement, feminism still faces many problems today.

To begin with, we're dealing with multiple issues: sexual assaults, domestic violence, inheritance laws, access to health and education, sex-selective abortions, female infanticide, custodial rape, dowry harassment, equal wage, gender stereotypes . . . I could go on and on. The battles we face are endless.

India's inherent heterogeneity has led to multiple patriarchies, which has led to multiple feminisms. Feminism in India does not abide by a singular narrative, which leads to dissension within ranks and outside. This weakens the movement. Even if my feminism is not your feminism, it is still feminism. We are united by a singular cause. Let's be supportive of one another.

Feminism in India has never been only about women. It has been intrinsically linked to colonialism, the independence movement and the consequent nation-building and development as well as modern-day conflicts. Due to this, the knowledge of what constitutes a 'woman' has never been explored fully. A woman is, therefore, seen either as an abla nari or krantikaari, a devi or dayan, a virgin or whore. She exists only in binaries. It's our country's greatest misfortune that our cultural norms have failed to honour women's fundamental rights.

Feminism has also been criticized for being the domain of the urban privileged, which is something it should not be. Feminism is not about preaching to the converted. It's about intersectionality and accessibility. It should include everyone: women, men, children, the LGBTQI, the ungendered, the Dalits, the urban, the rural . . . anyone who is human! Let's keep at it!

The other issue at hand is that of inclusion. Men are not seen as stakeholders in the feminist movement. In fact, it takes a rare man to call himself a feminist. The fault usually lies in the way they are raised and the cultural messaging they receive.

This is surprising. Men have historically been powerful allies in India's feminist movement. If Sarojini Naidu asked for women's voting rights, Raja Rammohan Roy abolished Sati. If Savitribai Phule fought for caste, education and social upliftment, Mahatma Gandhi started the Stree Shakti movement. Even in religion, Indian goddesses such as Durga, Saraswati and Laxmi are revered like the gods, as equals. Where did we lose our way?

That said, feminism is not about disrupting the socioeconomic balance but about restoring it. So, while women must be raised as equals to men, we cannot ignore our sons for our daughters, the way our daughters were ignored for our sons, for that would further perpetuate the cycle of discrimination—the very thing we're fighting against!

Therefore, feminism is about creating an equal society . . . not just for women, but also for men. It's about believing that women are equal to men—equal in access, opportunity, and respect. Feminism is saying that women should be paid the same as men, *and* that men shouldn't have to pick up each restaurant bill. It's saying that a woman can step out of the kitchen, *and* a man can step into the kitchen. It's saying that a woman can be an army jawan, *and* a man can be a Kathak dancer. It's about saying that a woman should not give dowry, *and* a man shouldn't be indicted in a false dowry case. It's about saying that a woman can fight, *and* a man can cry.

Feminism is not about women versus men, but women *and* men versus a system that is unfair, the system of patriarchy that has failed us all as human beings.

And being a feminist is being a (good) human. It's actually as simple as that!

In fact, I don't understand why everyone is *not* a feminist.

So, if you're sick of being seen in a gendered way, whether you're a woman or a man, young or old, lesbian or trans, Dalit or Brahmin; if you're tired of being boxed into a gender stereotype; if you want women to be safe and men to be sensitive; if you want to change the conversation, then be a proud feminist! Make some noise! Change the rules! Change the narrative! Change your legacy! Leave behind a better country for India's daughters *and* sons.

For when an individual changes, a family changes; when families change, society changes; when societies change, the nation changes, and then the world becomes a better place. And don't we all deserve to live in a better world?

Meghna Pant

Introduction

One has to be bold and fearless to start conversations on feminism, thanks to the intensely patriarchal society that India is. So many of us have heard the familiar refrains, 'do not raise your voice', 'sit daintily', 'be coy', 'do not raise your eyes' and 'do not talk back'. To be able to express one's opinion is a privilege. As a journalist and a woman raised in an open-minded family, these privileges were a given for me. Unfortunately, over the course of my twenty-year media career I came to realize that most Indian women are forced to hide their real selves behind the roles that society imposes on them, no matter how affluent or impoverished their circumstances might be or how educated they might be.

Sexism can be found motivating many given, unsaid/said everyday rules—breastfeeding in public is considered scandalous and deplorable; the kitchen is the sanctimonious space assigned to women; a man shouting in an office is thought to be 'in control' while a woman instructing loudly is judged to be graceless and so on. This observation urged me to think of creating safe spaces to initiate conversations on rights, sexism, feminism, behaviour, discrimination and class, and to enable people with an opinion but no mic to speak up. We need to talk about these issues. No, not behind closed doors but out in the open. Loudly, clearly and together. This led to the birth of SheThePeople, India's first channel for women, which has championed feminism in its true spirit and opened many conversations through its initiative called 'Feminist Rani'.

Feminist Rani, the book, encapsulates fourteen of these bold conversations with courageous people, not shy to talk about their deepest fears and influences. The chapters on Kalki Koechlin, Aditi Mittal, Shree Gauri Sawant, Gul Panag, Rana Ayyub, Deepa Malik and Aarefa Johari have been written by Meghna, while I have penned the ones on Gurmehar Kaur, Ankhi Das, Sapna Bhavnani, Sorabh Pant, Tanmay Bhat, Malishka Mendonsa and Rohini Shirke.

These include discussions about claiming one's body, environment, views, vagina, and making one's choices. Student activist Gurmehar Kaur asks us not to reduce women to reserved compartments and seats in metro trains and buses. Women's equality should be about equal access to opportunities, and not about queues to enter a monument, she maintains. Radio jockey Malishka Mendonsa calls for female friendships to thrive and not scrutinized by men and women. Beekeeper Rohini Shirke discusses her resolve to find respect and financial independence. Each interview is fierce and brutally honest about dealing with shame and the resurrection of one's self.

Feminist Rani debunks the stereotypes associated with the word feminism by providing fresh interpretations.

It urges one to believe that there is no one definition of feminism; it comes draped in ambition, vulnerability, power, fundamental rights, motherhood, bachelorhood, wealth, opportunity (or the lack of it) and depravity. It's ultimately about creating access to opportunity and having agency.

This book is a rich and powerful source of experiences and stories by people not afraid to be different, to voice an opinion, question current beliefs, and posit a new, more inclusive future. Regardless of their gender, complexion and sexual preferences, these people believe in equality of all. For them, feminism isn't a poster on the wall, it is an unseen, empowering belief and force.

Personally, writing this book has been a journey into myself. For me, feminism is the right to be who you want to be. It is a movement that not only champions gender equality but also finds ways in which women can empower themselves to become physically, intellectually, culturally, financially and emotionally independent.

Shaili Chopra

Kalki Koechlin

Actor, Writer, Activist

'The biggest problem with marriage, especially for a woman, is the idea of ownership: that you belong to me; I own you. Once I got married, I was only invited to the things that Anurag was invited to. People would say, "Call Anurag's wife." They wouldn't say, "call Kalki" or "call Kalki's husband". In marriage, a woman becomes the weaker sex, even if her husband doesn't want her to. This happens because of the way society has built the institution,' Kalki Koechlin tells me.

It's surprising that the agency of women in marriage, or the lack thereof, is a phenomenon from which not even filmstars are immune. There is no way for me to imagine this. Like most people, I have nothing to do with Bollywood except to appreciate or censure it. It's a world I can inhabit only from the outside. But I can surmise this little thing: as someone who was married to acclaimed director Anurag Kashyap, and went through a highly publicized divorce, Kalki understands the role of women in love, relationships, marriage, divorce and conscious uncoupling.

She looks at the rustling leaves of the yellow flame tree outside her window and adds, 'I don't think I'll get married again.'

I try not to show my surprise.

We're sitting on a large couch at her home, which is stripped down, unpretentious and minimalistic, like her performances. She's wearing a simple *ganji* and jeans, devoid of shoes, make-up and jewellery. Her thoughts, her home and her clothes are something entirely unexpected from a screen diva; yet, they befit her. I've known Kalki only a few minutes, but she strikes me as someone who doesn't require material wealth with which to fill her life. She's already filled it with self-reflection and thought.

She continues: 'Maybe I'll find a partner that I want to be with. But I'd want to respect the independence of that person and of myself, because it's as easy for me to own that person and want them to be mine completely. You have to let go of ego and say: "Okay, you don't belong to me, but I'm here and you're free to be with me and I'm free to be with you, and we dedicate a certain honesty to each other." I believe in honesty as the key to any relationship. Have complete honesty but keep your independence, keep separate friends, if you can afford it, keep a separate place, and keep some idea of life outside each other, so you're not putting all the pressure on each other.'

It's a balmy August afternoon in 2015 as Mumbai's rains beat a hasty retreat. Somewhere in the byelanes of Versova a temple bell rings, clear and crisp amid the noise of traffic, one can hear vegetable vendors and barking dogs. I take a sip of water and look at her.

Bugs Bunny meets Julia Roberts is how the *Chicago Sun-Times* described her character in *That Girl in Yellow Boots*. But to me, she's Audrey Hepburn in the twenty-first century: waiflike, elfin and self-assured. There is an effervescent and radiant quality to her.

'Women should not have a rulebook on how to live their life. We tend to lose ourselves when we look for approval from the outside. It's really about trying to be true to yourself and to be honest. I know that it's easier said than done. It's easy to be honest in public and in front of others, but to remain honest behind closed doors is quite difficult. Put yourself in a home environment where you have to stand up to loved ones and disagree with those who you love. That's tough. Being honest is not easy. We all have a public persona that is lovable but to remain honest to yourself at all times is what women could look into.'

'Women should strive to live an authentic life,' she adds sincerely. 'Why do we need approval from others?'

I agree. But for women in India this is the most difficult part, as it's been for Kalki too. Like many Indian women who don't follow a prescribed patriarchal path, Kalki has spent her entire life breaking stereotypes and preconceived notions about her self, her agency and her identity. She has often spoken about the fact that people made assumptions about her when they thought that she was white, when she became an actress and when she got divorced. She broke through that noise and clutter to make choices that have made her one of India's most admired women. Is there poetic justice in all this?

'I don't know if it's justice, but it's a great relief to find myself in all of this. There's always the need to fit in, right? The struggle is to find your individual self. From childhood I've been the black sheep, although I was white (laughs). I was the one blonde girl with all my South Indian friends. I wanted to fit in so I spoke Tamil and not English. You naturally try to be "liked" and loved by people. I still want, of course, to be liked and loved by people, but instead of looking out, trying to find approval from everyone else, and losing out on the person that I am, I want to look into myself. The last few years have been about working on myself.'

Kalki talks to me with that same sense of abandonment that characterizes her performances, leaving everything else of herself behind. She's effortless, in the moment and inclusive. I can sense this in the way she lets her teeth show when she smiles.

'Because of circumstances . . . coming out of a marriage . . . I found myself alone after a very long time. I had to fill up that empty space somehow. I didn't want to fill it up by going crazy and getting drunk, or by surrounding myself with people. I chose the introverted version of filling up myself by spending more time at home, more time with the family, going away somewhere and reading books. It proved to really fulfil me. I'm happy I went through that journey.'

There it is—that mulish determination that she translates so well on screen. If more women had the ability to watch their inner selves and stand by their choices and decisions, more women would be able to talk as sincerely, frankly and passionately as Kalki does. Her choices, body of work and sense of courage obviously stem from recognizing what is unique within her and not letting go of that uniqueness.

This is of course counterintuitive in her world—in society, in Bollywood, in this city of Mumbai. I ask her how tough is it to be authentic in a country where women are told to follow cookie-cutter lives and to inhabit an industry that is flushed with artifice. Is she really so courageous?

'I don't have this amazing courage or anything,' she tells me, like many strong women have told me. 'You reach a point in your life when you don't have a choice. I'm lucky I reached that point quite early in my life, where I've exhausted all those things that convention tells you to do: have a job, a house, a family and kids. These are the things convention tells us are normal, and will make us successful or fit in. Once those are exhausted, people have their mid-life crisis, mostly in their forties or fifties, when their kids have gone away they wonder what life will be about now and what else is there?'

To be original in a world occupied by cloned perfection must have been tough. But Kalki did it. She found her place under the bright arc lights, the hallowed paths of glitzy Bollywood, the hullabaloo of its charms and deceptions. Her characters soaked us with their infinite warmth, childlike vulnerabilities and ancient wisdom. She essayed roles that became her. She owned them. From the role of a prostitute, to a girl afflicted with cerebral palsy, to a hand-job-giving masseuse, she has challenged the status quo, pushed the envelope, and extended boundaries to new places. 'For me this has, firstly, been about being authentic and not stereotyping, and secondly about not repeating myself and staying in the comfort zone. As an actor, I'm trying to grow and do things that scare and challenge me.'

The journey she speaks of may be one of the reasons that Kalki has been described as 'a rare, unabashed feminist voice among our celebrities today'. In a nation with poor knowledge of feminist history and poor understanding of the feminist movement, this is a big deal. What does feminism mean to her?

'I think a feminist is somebody who believes in women being humans,' Kalki says, adding that the word 'feminism' is about all humans being equal and respecting one another. She loves being a feminist but is threatened by the thought that India has come to believe in a 'militant idea' of the concept and therefore ruined it. 'They think that a feminist has to be a "man-hater", or a lesbian, or aggressive. I don't think that's a feminist,' she adds. 'It's only that we live in a patriarchal society, and therefore, the word feminism has to be used as a counter to patriarchy. But feminism is about being equal. The word used should be "equalist", as it's about all humans being equal and respecting each other for that.'

Has she always been a feminist?

'I didn't take a conscious decision to find myself as one. Due to my family and my spiritual background of growing up in the Sri Aurobindo Ashram (Pondicherry), this sense of discovery has been ingrained in me from an early age. I've realized that, in life, there are so many things that we use to fill up the empty spaces. You have to strip yourself from all this. Ask yourself that if I'm

Kalki Koechlin

stripped of my wealth, my success, my friends and my
loved ones, what do I have left? Recognize what that is.
That is what's worth fighting for. Because that's all you
have left, that's all you came into the world with and all
you will leave with. I know this sounds philosophical but
it's something that has stayed with me.'

She smiles gently and runs her fingers through her
auburn hair.

'As a result, I'm a fuller and more understanding
person. As a teenager I was quite a rebel. I wanted to be
an arguer or the one who didn't agree. Now—more and
more—I want to understand the other person's point of
view, why somebody is conservative when I'm liberal,
and to come to a meeting point. We all live in the same
world and we all share the same space. If we don't try
to understand each other, there will always be wars and
disputes. So the people I fear most, or hate most, are the
ones I want to confront and understand, and figure out
why we've become so distant. Feminism is really about
being a human being who is constantly rethinking her
existence and trying to grow.'

Clearly, her life is a departure from the female
prototype deeply set in the Indian psyche, of this self-
denying and self-sacrificing chaste Sati Savitri. In the larger
context of our society, women have been conditioned
and programmed to be servile in many ways—to please
our fathers, our husbands, our brothers and our sons.
We've been given the odious task of bettering our men,
our household, our family and our children, if only we
sacrifice and compromise and adjust. What kind of life
are you leading as a woman in India if you say I will not

sacrifice, I will not compromise, I will not be subservient, and I will not adjust?

Is there a price Kalki has had to pay for being unconventional?

'No, I've not had to pay a heavy price. In fact, rather than feel the pressure to keep doing something, I have retained my freedom and my ability to pick and choose. Of course, people have tried to stereotype me. Take my films, for example. After *Dev.D* I got only prostitute roles for a year and I had to keep saying no to them. After *That Girl in Yellow Boots* the hand-job jokes came on Twitter in a big way. You have to face all that noise. But it's very short-lived if you realize that you're only as new as your newest film. People remember *Margarita, with a Straw*; the year before that they remembered *Yeh Jawaani Hai Deewani,* next year they'll remember something else. You have to look beyond the period of initial reactions and recognize that there's a bigger body of work and an effort to do something bigger.'

No wonder, that unlike most Bollywood actors, Kalki also inhabits the world of theatre. She has her own theatre company Little Productions. I've watched her essay different roles underscoring human absurdities in the play *Trivial Disasters,* where she created her own identity as well as she does on screen. It's no surprise then that she's earned rave reviews for writing and directing a new play called *The Living Room* that has the signature black humour reminiscent of the inimitable Woody Allen.

'Theatre has been a backbone for whenever I've run out of film work. After *Dev.D* I didn't have film industry work for one-and-a-half years. It would have been easy for me to go into depression, doubt myself and say, 'Oh my god . . . I'm never going to get work . . . I'm a crap actor.' I would have gotten into that zone if it weren't for my theatre friends, who said, 'Let's do something! Let's write a script!' That urge to create has come from theatre. Even now I do a new play every two years. There's also a natural dip and cycle in films. I'll do two-three films together, and then nothing for nine months. There's a boom in the work and then there's a slow period. In that slow period, as an actor, I don't want to lose touch with my craft. If you're a musician you have to handle your instrument every day; that's your *riyaaz*. As an actor it's very difficult to practise your instrument of acting every day, unless you dress as Charlie Chaplin and go with your hat on the streets (laughs). So theatre is my riyaaz.'

If theatre is a resurrection, then what is love? After all, the centrepiece of our human experience and emotions is love. To love and be loved is our greatest need and may well be the reason we were sent down here. Yet, as women inhabiting a world that is at once modern and traditional, love is the one thing we neither understand nor do correctly. As an artist, Kalki is especially sensitive to this emotion as she's experienced, engaged and expressed it in myriad ways and in its different shades. As a feminist, what have been her experiences with matters of the heart?

'That's a good question,' she says and pauses to reflect on her idea of relationships. 'Love is the most important aspect of being human, and the most beautiful thing about humans is our capacity to love. But women grow up with a Disney World idea of love, as I did, where we think we'll meet someone who will provide us with everything, and we'll live happily ever after as we walk into the sunset with Prince Charming. The person you're with has to live up to so many expectations: they have to be your friend, your father, your mother, and your child. They're supposed to be every aspect to you. That's unfair. As a society we've grown into this very insular idea of love and relationships, where your husband or wife becomes your only pillar of strength and everyone else is secondary. That's also unfair since we need many pillars of strength. So many of us disconnect from our family or community or friends when we get married, and that's really sad because no human being—however perfect, however nice—can provide you with everything you need. It's not possible. We love in so many forms. For me love is about building those pillars of strength in all aspects. A relationship for me is about finding love and respect in all walks of life.'

It's interesting that the *Margarita, with a Straw* actor believes that one human being cannot provide a woman with everything and she needs to nurture and build 'pillars of strength in every aspect', which includes friends, family and work colleagues. It also reminds me of a line from one of Kalki's movies, *That Girl in Yellow Boots*, where she quotes *Alice in Wonderland,* saying that she can't find that one person she's looking for, not because she's getting smaller, but because the world is getting bigger. It's poignant and honest, especially for modern love when we have so many options, yet at no point in history have so many people been single. Seeing all this, does Kalki still believe in love?

Kalki pauses and looks outside. Sunbeams stream in through the curtains, swirling dust motes in their wake. A yellow flower from the flame tree falls gently to her windowsill.

'The idea of romance is fading away,' she says poignantly. 'The idea of waiting and hoping for somebody to come and save you . . . your Prince Charming . . . is a myth. Now I'm freeing myself and running away from the Disney idea of love. When I meet a guy I tell myself, "No! He is not Prince Charming. He's not going to solve all my problems." I don't put all my hopes on one man and expect him to fulfil them. That's a conscious thing I'm doing. This way you let yourself grow and you let the other person grow. That's when you start loving each other in a different way, and in a much bigger way. It liberates you from the little things, the finicky things we argue about. Love then becomes about the bigger person you're trying to be and what you're trying to do in this world.'

And what is she trying to do in this world?

'I don't want to be remembered only for my work, I want to be remembered for who I am. We actors love our work because it will live on after us; like Smita Patil's films will be watched for long because of the kind of work she did. But that work wouldn't have happened if it weren't for the persona that's behind it and the person that she was. I too want to be remembered for the person that I am.'

There is really no other way. She's inspired us through her layered performances and through her layered life. She has had the courage to think and act differently and—more importantly—to embrace her peculiarities.

As she sees me out the front door, I look out of Kalki Koechlin's window one last time. When I think of her now, I think of the sky. Everybody else is like the clouds. They come and go. They pass. But she stays, etched in our collective conscious not only for the brilliant roles she's played on screen, but also for charting a course for women in a way only a true feminist can: through merit and example.

Gurmehar Kaur

Author, Activist, Youth Leader

'I used to hate Muslims because I thought all Muslims were Pakistanis. When I was six years old, I tried to stab a woman in a burka. Pakistan didn't kill my dad, war did.' An eighteen-year-old Delhi University student took to social media to campaign for peace between India and Pakistan. What she got in return was another war. A social-media post turned Gurmehar into enemy number one for the majority of right-wing trolls, and they took to their timelines to criticize her. This was just because she had expressed her opinion on Pakistan. Gurmehar lost her father in the 1999 Kargil war, and has a point of view on Indo-Pak relations. The online skirmishes turned ugly as she started getting rape and murder threats, and politicians started questioning her right to express herself. Despite being a martyr's daughter, no one was willing to accept that she could have an independent opinion on how the India–Pakistan relationship. Instead, her innocent call for peace was tagged 'anti-national' by some people.

When her dad died, Gurmehar, now twenty, was two years old. Her father, Captain Mandeep Singh (thirty), was posted in 4 Rashtriya Rifles (RR) in Kupwara when militants stormed his camp in August 1999. He was killed in the gun battle that followed. Gurmehar's life changed. He used to call her Gulgul.

17

She remembers nothing of when the news came. 'We were in Jalandhar—my father's brothers, his dad and my mom. I was there too. My sister was three months old.' Theirs was a joint family; her father's brothers were young—nineteen and twenty-two, respectively—and studying at the time. 'My mother [Rajvinder] and father's dad were the key people at home when dad was travelling.'

A few years after her dad's death, Gurmehar says, they moved into her maternal grandmother's home in Jalandhar—she, her mom and her sister. Her mom had to take up a job after her father's death. She got a transferable job in the revenue services. 'Good thing was that even if she was posted out of Jalandhar, it would still be in Punjab. So we didn't quite keep moving with her every time.' Her mom now lives in Amritsar.

Gurmehar studied at St Joseph's Convent School in Jalandhar on the cantonment road but didn't finish her schooling there. Instead, she opted to learn tennis and got inducted into a tennis boarding school in Ludhiana. As a result, she was home-schooled for classes X, XI, XII. 'I grew up doing what I wanted. My mom made it happen. Tennis was my calling, and my family didn't hold me back. They encouraged me.'

This freedom of choice came from growing up in a house full of women. There was no space for patriarchy. 'I've grown up in a household where the head of the family was my mother. I went to an all-girls school where the head of my school was a nun.' So, she says, in her formative years, she saw women being in charge.

She never even needed to think what feminism really was. It was the world she grew up in. 'There was never a day when I decided that I will be a feminist. I grew up in a women's world by default.' It was when she read and heard what people said that she was introduced to the world's interpretation of it. For most people in society, she recounts, it is an awkward tag. She noted how society expected women to be different and follow a certain way of life, be more subservient to men, not have a voice. Not be bold or brave. 'During my teens, I understood that in this way of life, women will always be second-class citizens, no matter which strata of society they came from, and this was when I knew for a fact that I wanted to work towards the kind of world and life I grew up in.' Interestingly in her own home, she saw the reaction to feminism vary and perhaps grow. 'For them, it was taking a stand. It was the need to prove themselves every time. For us, it was what we were born with.'

Does Gurmehar Kaur have her own definition of feminism?

'For me, feminism has a very simple definition. To be a feminist is to work towards a future that doesn't abide by the rules of a patriarchal world, where women need to be feminine, docile and take care of the household, while men need to be the exact opposite—masculine and strong. Feminism equals the end of patriarchy.'

Once she arrived at the tennis academy, she took to it instantly because it fostered a friendlier environment than her school. She says it also stood for many of her own principles. It was an equal space, she says. 'I was talent playing against talent. Not a woman against man, or younger against more experienced. I beat boys by having superior skill. Let's not forget, it is also the sport where Billie Jean King challenged an ATP men's player to a match and won it. It was called the Battle of the Sexes, and it proved that women aren't weak.'

Tennis brought her resolve and a go-getter attitude, but little did she know it would also produce her weakest moment. At eighteen, when she was nearly ready to take up the sport professionally, she suffered a severe knee injury that put her off the sport for years. Gurmehar plunged into depression, and spent hours in bed. 'It was heartbreak. I wouldn't get out of my bed, and ate chips. I was so negative.' She calls it her most nervous phase. 'All your life you were practising for one thing and it was gone suddenly. I still find that so tough. I wanted to be a professional tennis player.' Luckily for her, tennis also had the answers.

She read about Maria Sharapova and her choppy life—raised by a single parent, facing injury many times over and failing a drug test, taking it all head-on to come out shining. 'The woman doesn't give up. As a tennis student, I kept her go-getting instinct in my head.'

'I overcame that negative phase—and that gave proof of my capability. I was brave. There was a voice in my head. The same one that made me keep playing tennis. Because I was an athlete for so long, I knew that time wouldn't roll back. You set goals, you achieve them. At some point, I stood up and said I had to finally take my life in my control. And so I did.'

Gurmehar says just like sport is an equalizer, expression too needs to be on that plank. 'Feminism, as a result for me, is a lot to do with tennis.'

In 2016, Gurmehar came to the University of Delhi and joined Lady Shri Ram College (LSR). She picked English honours. The transition was new. What changed from Punjab to Delhi? The shift brought her a greater sense of confidence and freedom. And a world view, she says. 'Convent schooling teaches you to be so competitive. That was my experience. All-girls schools can be very cut-throat. I hated school. LSR didn't have any snark. You could wear *suit-salwar* and no one would call you a *behenji*. You could wear a miniskirt and no one would pass judgements. That was liberating.' She says her college was an inspiration on many counts—from being able to speak at public forums, the diversity of thought, 'that sense of breaking boundaries and exposing myself to being part of something bigger. In school, I was lonely for the most part, but here I felt there were others who believe in a common cause.' She credits the move to Delhi with giving her wind beneath her activist wings. She spent time working with not-for-profits, speaking to and bringing people together on subjects of gender equality, peace and student life. Although it meant Gurmehar spent a lot of time outside of college, she would 'attend a variety of events, speak and discuss with other activists across colleges. I was part of Pinjra Tod as well'. Pinjra Tod is a Delhi University movement by young women to oppose gender bias in hostel rules, which mostly insist women should return to colleges by a certain time while men have no restrictions.

But the activist in Gurmehar was questioned (and threatened) in February 2017, when she stood up to violence against students in colleges. She had launched a social media campaign against the Akhil Bharatiya Vidyarthi Parishad (ABVP), which allegedly clashed with students of a college in Delhi University. Her message, 'I am not afraid of ABVP', went viral on social media, provoking kudos as well as rape threats. Celebrities such as cricketer Virender Sehwag and actor Randeep Hooda also wrote against her, mocking her sense of nationalism. Politicians attacked her. 'The most significant and life-altering experience was when I stood up against violence against students on university campuses. What struck me was how no one looked at me as a student standing up for other students, but as a martyr's daughter, which is why I felt the need to write a blog where I say "while my father is a martyr and I'm his daughter, I'm not your martyr's daughter".' An excerpt of the blog is published below with Gurmehar's permission.

Am I who the trolls think I am?
Am I what the media portrayed me as?
Am I what those celebrities think of me?

No, I can't be any of that. That girl you saw flashing all over your television screens, holding a placard in hand, eyebrows raised, gaze fixed at the tiny round lens of a cellphone camera, definitely looked like me. The intensity of her thoughts that reflected in the picture definitely had traces of me. She looked fiery, I relate to that but then the 'Breaking news headlines' told a different story. The headlines were not me.

The streaks of this dialogue and confidence were all over Gurmehar's campaign for peace. It exposed the intolerance of many in society to understand, appreciate and empathize with another viewpoint on violence, harmony and war. 'A twenty-year-old's call for peace and protest against violence could create such a stir that it forced me to think,' Gurmehar reflects on the moral values of India's youth, and how the world turned against her for voicing a view on India and Pakistan. 'People told me that my basic moral values had disrupted the country's political narrative.' She insists her campaign was not about political parties, but about students and to keep the campus safe from violence and threats. 'No matter which organization you are associated with, you cannot threaten women with rape. That cannot happen,' she says.

The voices, she says, luckily weren't those of trolls alone. There were millions who hailed and backed Gurmehar. 'Social media has given each and every woman a voice,' she says. It has liberated Indian women who grow up in households where they are taught to be quiet, to not talk over adults, especially male adults, and not to be too opinionated. 'For young girls, social media acts as a platform where they can say things they might not be able to say in their homes, and find a community of like-minded women.'

However, dealing with such intense media scrutiny and spotlight wasn't something Gurmehar had imagined. 'I remember it came as a shock to me. I was lost. But by the second day, I realized admitting that the media and public would cast aspersions [on my character] and extrapolate that I was lost. So tennis came to the rescue. All my early lessons were useful. In my head, I went back to being an athlete.

You need to know how to shut yourself to what you don't want to hear. That was the best thing for me. I wanted to divert attention from myself to the students.'

Gurmehar was named 'freedom of speech warrior' by *TIME* in 2017. She believes women need a voice, one that's loud and clear. 'When my world became full of violence and hatred, I cut myself off from the world,' Gurmehar was scared and she admitted her world was shaken up. 'I was scared I won't have friends any more. Would people talk to me or not? I was forced to even wonder if I would be able to complete my education.' She took a break and went off to meditate at a *vipassana* centre. She returned clear-headed.

'Post vipassana. I took the narrative in my own hands. I didn't want to go down Google history as a controversy that was a flash in the pan. At the end of the day, I had a cause that I believed in. I didn't want someone to tell my story, instead I wanted to tell it myself.'

As an activist, she wants to be able to start these conversations in places where it's hard to have these conversations. She raises important questions. Could we begin a dialogue where conversations on sexual harassment, and the concept of feminism are put into focus? Where they are not reduced to reserved seats in metro trains or buses? Where women's equality is about equal access to opportunities, and not about queues to enter a monument? 'In an ideal world, everyone should be able to do whatever they want. That kind of true freedom is what I look at and aim for.'

At an early age, the experience—the good, bad and ugly—of speaking up, has both taught her a lot and brought her access to people, thinkers, and public speakers. It has inspired her to pursue a life in public service. 'I think I aged a decade over those three days. I have a defined direction I want to follow. I know I will be in the public eye. It's not so much about journalism, writing, or joining a magazine. I am now in public spaces, so I want to keep my career options open. I want to pursue a career that aids politics and other public facing efforts I want to undertake.'

Her next focus is how her efforts could impact more people and society. 'While my friends are worried about semester exams, my worries are bigger. I want to do bigger projects.'

She talks about the right to express, and the need for us to speak up for peace. 'Words are our superpower.' She isn't new to them. While growing up, she was a voracious reader, influenced by women who had severe experiences. 'Louisa Alcott's *Little Women* was among the first I read. It was fascinating to me that her story was so similar to mine. In the book, the father's gone away to war. That was the first time I realized my family isn't unusual as people do have lives like mine. It made me think I had a connection. Sometimes even when you are in an ecosystem, you do feel lonely and scared. That book changed my life.'

The Diary of a Young Girl by Anne Frank was another one; it seems like a great prototype for Gurmehar to write her book on because it's a memoir of a young person's life. 'I read it when I was eleven. I realized there were no such books in the Indian context or I hadn't read any of them by then. It was an inspiration and I thought I could write something on those lines.'

Things came full circle for Gurmehar at twenty, when after all the controversy around her social campaign, she decided to write her own book. 'I knew I wanted to write a book after I read Anne Frank's *Diary*. It was my first motivation. I didn't want to lose the memories of my father, and wanted to document his life and ours without him.' She started penning down her thoughts when she was twelve. 'I finally wrote it now. At twenty. The incidents of February 2017 didn't change the content, but it added context to my experiences.'

The book is about her grandmother, Amarjeet, her mom and the lives they had, being breadwinners and nurturers. 'My grandmother lost her husband really early, when my mom was just nine. He was an engineer who died in an on-site accident. Grandmother raised two daughters by herself. The story repeated itself with my mom, who had to raise two daughters. It was painful. My family had to survive. Mothers took on male roles even before such prescribed roles were questioned and feminism was talked about.' This was a struggle, especially in a small town like Jalandhar. But they came out as heroes. Everyday heroes, says Gurmehar, who are an inspiration for all.

The next twenty years for Gurmehar will be powerful, enriched with experience and challenges. Even with the small amount of public exposure she has had so far, she's learnt an important lesson as a woman—'you are on your own'.

Sapna Bhavnani

Philanthropist, Hair Stylist, Rape Survivor

'We drew a portrait of mother earth holding her naked bosoms. She had roots and was a fruit-bearing tree. We knew children, including boys, would look at it. This mural was going to be on the village school wall. On the entrance door we painted a weighing scale—something villagers often drew—for grains or paper or whatever. I made a man and woman on it, and kept the scale equal,' Sapna Bhavnani shares her feminist effort at bringing gender equality to a small village in Maharashtra.

These scenes were very different from her busy, modern, bulb-lit hair salon, where she styles people like cricketer M.S. Dhoni (remember his Mohawk?), actor Priyanka Chopra and many other celebrities. In the village, men and women didn't care for her celeb status; they were only interested in her objectives. Sapna was in Palegaon, Maharashtra, to change ground realities for them.

'The men in the village held a conference. [They were] upset about this mural and [wanted to] debate whether this is what their children should see. But the teacher didn't get flustered at all. She was supportive and went on to tell the villagers to look at the mural in the *correct* way. To know that it's important for children to see the mother as tree and bearer of all that they get. She said to the people, if you look at it negatively, you interpret it as bad. If you see it positively, you will interpret it as good. The teacher herself was a strong woman, coming out as feminist in the village.'

Sapna works with two villages in Maharashtra—Johar and Palegaon. The latter she has adopted and returns to often. That is where the school is. It's an Adivasi village. In Johar she, along with an NGO, set up a women's centre. 'The more I worked with women in villages, the more I realized how empowered the women really are over there. In Johar, we raised funds for ten sewing machines. We set up the centre there.' She recalls that while the women sang and welcomed them, the men brought her the biggest surprise. 'The most feminist thing I heard that day, and it stays with me, came from a man. He said to me, "I get all my power from my women. So if my women are empowered, imagine how much power I will get." Sapna says it was the most logical thing she had ever heard. Even better, he was a village teacher and that was even more reassuring. 'My experiences in villages have empowered me even more because every time I go there, no one ever seems to judge me because my appearance or my hair. I get more judged in cities but in villages the women accept me for who I am. That's the core and essence of feminism; where you don't judge other women, and I have learnt that from village folks.'

Sapna has a unique personality. Her hair colour changes often, from pink to gold with a punk or rock look. Her body is covered in tattoos and piercings, and her dresses reflect the vibrant individual she is. She prefers wearing black, but can surprise you when she walks into a gender debate.

On one of the episodes of Feminist Rani, she walked in boldly wearing a pink dress, triggering 'hmmms' in a roomful of people waiting to hear her thoughts on feminism. The baby pink outfit clashed subtly with her fully tattooed body, putting her body language ahead of feminist talk. 'Feminists don't have to wear black. I am a feminist in pink! I am in love with the feminine, and everything can be feminist about feminine.' With that one sentence, she started deconstructing and rebuilding the idea that we call feminism.

'I think I was born a feminist. I don't wake up every day and say, as a woman I should do this. I think of myself as someone who wants something, and will go out and get it. It's about equal rights for me. To me feminism is like masculinity is to a man; he isn't asked what it means to be masculine on a daily basis.'

* * *

Sapna grew up in Mumbai in a Sindhi family. Her father owned a cabaret joint called Blue Nile and a Chinese restaurant called Wongs. She was raised in Bandra, and went to school there. She was a good student, but by her own admission, she 'discovered' boys in Class VII. Her exposure to the world of films, fashion and style drew her away from academics even more. 'When I was fourteen, I used to talk to boys, drive motorcycles, smoke cigarettes, and people in Bandra would often call me a whore because of those things. I never understood the term back then.' Her father passed away in a sudden turn of events when Sapna was just eighteen. This affected 'daddy's girl' a great deal, and her life was plunged into commotion. The family's financial condition suffered. Sapna says she became erratic in attending school and started having disagreements and fights with her mom.

'After my father's death I moved to Chicago, where there were so many like me, and it gave me the freedom to get inked, experiment with my hair and just be myself,' she says about her early days in America. Her aunt had helped her move there, and Sapna enrolled in Barat College to study marketing and communication. Alongside, she pursued styling and hair-dressing, and since there were many bills to pay, Sapna waited tables at an Italian restaurant.

'One Christmas Eve in Chicago, I walked out of a bar alone late at night in a short dress and red lipstick. I was twenty-four and had been drinking, when from a dumpster, a group of guys walked up to me and put a gun to my head asking me to give them blow jobs, which eventually led to gang rape. I remember walking home, shivering and pushing this incident to the back of my mind for years and never letting it break my spirit—I still wear short dresses and the brightest red on my lips.'

Sapna says she first shared this experience in the play *Nirbhaya* in 2013. The play was based on the gruesome gang rape and murder of a girl in Delhi in 2012 that had made global headlines. Later, she shared this online in a post with Humans of Bombay.

For most of us who are traumatized after hearing of such horrific stories, or being groped in public spaces, Sapna is a role model. She says she regained her sense of self, her dignity, by letting her mind forget the incident. 'I didn't call for the punishment of my perpetrators.' After so many years of hiding the incident inside her, Sapna spoke about it only a few years ago. Why now?

During the talk on Feminist Rani, she was vociferous that women should not be pressurized into speaking out about their problems. 'Speaking out, or not, is a personal choice that does not make a woman less of a feminist,' she said. She adds that some of the strongest women are the ones who keep silent and tolerate the many issues inflicted upon them via patriarchy.

'It's because sometimes there are things that are beyond your control. We live in a world where everyone stresses the importance of voicing yourself or walking out of tough situations, but I just want to say this—no one wants to be beaten up, raped or sell their bodies. It took me twenty years to voice my incident, but for me, a woman keeping it all within her because she has no other choice isn't a sign of weakness—it's a mark of strength, and something we need to start respecting.' She asserts that the biggest lesson she learnt was to speak her heart out, speak the truth. 'And the world came to support me and talk to me. Never not speak the truth.'

After the incident in Chicago, Sapna returned to India. She suffered three failed marriages. Her first, with a German national, ended because his family was apparently racist. Her second marriage was to an Indian man for whom she relocated from the USA to India, but Sapna says he was violent. Her third marriage, she admits, split due to her.

For someone who has gone through three botched relationships, she has fought back and turned her life upside down to find purpose. In a country like India where the agency of women is defined as beginning and ending in marriage, Sapna said that she has de-linked herself from the institution.

'People look at me as a forty-five-year-old single woman with no husband or child, and call me a *bechari*. Such terms need to go. Call me a *krantikaari* instead!' she said to resounding applause.

Sapna is among the early champions of Stop Acid Attacks, a Facebook community dedicated to fighting acid attacks on women. She says it started when she met a person called Aseem in the Bigg Boss House, and she credits him for showing her the real meaning of feminism. 'It was him and his roommate, Alok, who were moved and passionate about the impact acid attacks have on women. I got involved to spread the word.' When she first met the women, she was uncertain and didn't know if she should look at them. She didn't know how to begin the conversation. 'I kept looking at them but had so many questions in my head. But the women just embraced me and we got talking.' These meetings changed her understanding of beauty, and how she thought about her work at her salon. 'I have been battling the question that does a salon instil a false sense of beauty? I have been asking that to myself for ten years now.' These women are warriors, Sapna says. 'As a [rape] survivor, I feel I still have an identity. But these women should be called warriors because they don't have their original physical identity. They don't have the face they knew themselves. I salute them.'

The Stop Acid Attacks campaign took off as it gathered steam online. It was a big effort, and people got to know about it through digital media. Sapna says digital and social media have transformed the opportunities for women. 'SheThePeople and Feminist Rani are in the forefront of putting digital ahead as a tool for women's empowerment. It showed me a perspective like nothing before. Even for women who want to sit at home and work online. The world has just opened up to the next level. There is something for everyone to do.'

In the end, Sapna Bhavnani will be known for a lot of things. Being a celebrity stylist, transforming Dhoni's hair style, the badass in *Bigg Boss*, her bold statements, her wicked tattoos, but what makes her a hero of the future is her ability to live her life on her own terms. For finding comfort in who she is. She says it's hard for her to forgive herself for staying silent for so many decades but wants every woman with a voice to speak up. There is respect in silence but resurrection in speaking up.

Aditi Mittal

Comedian

I speak to her once she's off stage. The floodlights have dimmed and the applause can no longer be heard. Over brownies and biryani—both of which she's stellar at making—we discuss quotidian things: men, dating and comedy.

I look at the purple streaks in her hair that she distractedly plays with. Her voice cracks when she tells me that my stories are the only things that make her cry. I up the ante. I tell Aditi Mittal that she's one of the few people who can make me laugh. She smiles. She hears this, almost every day. Why wouldn't she? She's among the country's top stand-up comedians and probably the funniest woman in India today. Her name is synonymous with comedy, and with success.

In a country where female comedians shape-shift into overweight sidekicks proven utterly undesirable, or horny vamps bellowing histrionics, Aditi is neither, making her a trailblazer.

We turn to more sombre things; like how we negotiate being women in India.

Aditi Mittal's bespectacled, ebullient face becomes serious.

Gender-linked pejoratives are tough to imagine when you're looking from a place of power. Not so with Aditi. She's broken the ceilings that prevented women from entering and staying in the predominantly male stand-up comedy scene. She's turned a one-man show into a one-woman show. The battles she's fought give her humour the edge that struggle demands. After all, stand-up is not just the ability to make people laugh, it is also the ability to transcend experiences and see things for what they are.

'When I started doing comedy I was told that a woman doing comedy is supposed to be as rare as a monkey doing Shakespeare,' she says. 'But I really didn't know it was a big deal. Nobody told me I couldn't do it, so I just went about doing what everybody else was doing. It's only as I gain distance from that time that I'm able to find the vocabulary for the experiences I was going through.'

Humour lacerates, not just the audience, but also the performers. Aditi soon learnt that things were not easy, especially for female comedians.

'When I started comedy, the one thing that surprised me was that there was so little in that narrative of funny things that happen to women. We women are taught to take ourselves 100 per cent seriously. So people would say, "Oh, you do your comedy from a woman's point of view," and I would respond, "Who else's point of view can I do it from?"'

Therefore, a comic look at the urban woman's existentialist dilemmas became fodder for Aditi. She was aware that while men had their humour described as political, observational or satirical, everything that came out of a woman's mouth was lumped into her gender. Discussing rape, dowry deaths, street harassment or even sanitary napkins was deemed as disruptive and brash. That didn't stop her. She wanted to establish that there is no such thing as 'female humour'. It is observational humour that reveals experiences specific to women.

'The first time I went up on stage, I realized that people may not have heard many jokes from a female perspective,' says Aditi. 'I also realized that stereotypes are still the biggest laughs. In a comedy club if you say that Punjabis are loud and Gujaratis are cheap, people love it! You have to give the audience a little bit of what they're used to before you take them on that journey where you want to take them. Once they're warmed up, you talk to them about the things that really matter to you. Since these stereotypes have existed for so long, they're ripe for parody.'

By invoking gender stereotypes, comedians like Aditi are renegotiating social norms and deconstructing biases.

Gender essentialism has become a common thread in Mittal's work and identity.

But comedy in India is sexist. It is not friendly to women.

'Earlier I used to be included in stand-up comedy shows because sometimes, they just need a woman to "sexy up" things,' she says. 'And then I have had shows denied to me because *"yaar tum ladies ho, ye boys' college hai, tujhe maar dalenge"*. Often it's not economically viable to book me for travelling gigs in groups because I cannot share a room with the guys, and so one room has to be specifically reserved for me, which raises costs.'

Stand-up comedy, in particular, remains a boys' club: numerically and experientially. This power dynamic perpetuates gender discrimination.

'Very often I stand backstage in comedy clubs waiting to get on stage and I hear male comics say cringe-worthy things about women, calling them bitches, abusing them for having left them. The audience claps for them,' Aditi tells me. 'But I've gotten very different reactions from audience members for making the same material jokes as men do. Shouldn't I be given the same amount of immunity? I shouldn't have to face a disapproving or stunned audience. Instead, I am accused of making jokes that are male-bashing. And I say, "Get over yourself. I have several average jokes about aeroplane food as well. Men are not the only thing I talk about."'

Off-stage, and this to me is shocking, things don't get much better. In the guise of taking photographs after shows, Aditi tells me, many men rub their penis against her. 'My boob has been grabbed so many times, I fear I'm losing sensation in the area.' She's back, with that hard-hitting humour that lacerates. A humour deployed by a woman entering the pantheon of men.

I spend a lot of time with comedians. They're typically adorable megalomaniacs prone to bouts of melancholy and self-doubt. Not unlike writers, if one takes away adorability. So I am not surprised when she tells me that others tell her that 'she's only getting this much work because she's a woman'. Such reductionist attitudes have long been ascribed to women's success.

'Imagine hearing over and over again that my success is not because I'm funny, but because I'm a woman. In the past I've spent so much time crying in the St Andrew's Auditorium's ladies bathroom that now, even when I go there to pee, tears spring to my eyes.'

For a moment we're both in on the joke of how absurd this reality is. It's rare to hear the truth from women about the everyday violence they experience in public, and even rarer to hear about the emotional violence that takes place in the private space. It's sad to live in a world where even laughter cannot obviate inequalities. Still, I am glad that women like Aditi are not circumscribed by these notions. Instead, she uses her comedy to catalyse change.

'A large part of comedy is selling it. It's having the confidence. For men, the confidence comes faster. The journey towards the *same* point of confidence will be different for women. There's a lifetime of being told to sit down and be quiet and be minimized, that we have to get over. That does not happen quickly or easily.'

With this bravado, Aditi found that things slowly changed. 'Earlier I'd hear titters and tch, tch when I said something. This "disapproval" would rattle me. I'd think, "Should I go on?" But once the lights came on, I'd see that people were shaking with laughter and I realized they're enjoying it, and tch–tching at themselves for enjoying those jokes.'

Aditi used the combative and pre-emptive art form of stand-up to her favour. She became the stand-up artiste who attacked everything that surrounds the audience's life, while avoiding derision and inviting agreement.

To be a comic, she laughs and says, 'You have to possess stupidity and fearlessness. You have to be really stupid to be that fearless. And thick-skinned. Because it's going to punch you a lot before you stand up, and you have to be willing to take those punches and keep on wanting to stand up.'

The childhood of a girl makes her the woman she is today. I want to know who has formed and shaped Aditi's opinions to a force that they have now become.

Aditi says that she grew up in a typical middle-class Punjabi family.

'I come from a place of huge privilege in terms of the fact that as a middle-class child, I had access to a good education. My parents never stopped me from pursuing what I wanted. My only complaint with my parents is that they didn't fix my flat feet. I swear my brother has the shapeliest arches on his feet, and my feet look like they should be webbed. I think my parents anticipated that he would require getting into a pair of heels more than I did.'

We laugh. She adds that in this stratum, women are typically considered 'decorated pieces of excitement for the man'.

'We have always wanted our women to fit into the devi or the *dayan* dichotomy. First, you raise her up and put her up on a pedestal of "ma, behen, devi", etc., and then the second she diverts even a little bit from your idea of her, you happily murder her and say you're doing it for her honour. It's mind-boggling.' She pauses. 'We don't want to be your Madonna and we don't want to be your whore. We don't want to be your *ghar ki izzat* and we don't want to be your office *ki shaan*. We want to be us. Start seeing women as human beings. That would be awesome.'

I remember one of Aditi's most revelatory statements in an earlier interview, when she said: 'I've said no to several interviews when they begin their story with "Well, you know, with all the horrible stories about women coming out of India today, yours will be a positive one." It horrifies me that the fact that I've not been left dead in a ditch with my head chopped off in spite of speaking my mind, is a reason to celebrate.'

This lends a ring of truth to her.

In her household, issues like objectification, sexual violence and intimidation of women were discussed, along with the need to include men and have role models in the pursuit of feminism. Yet, of late, when we look around, more and more public figures have been denouncing feminism as an ideology. Concepts like 'meninism' and 'femi-nazi' have become popular buzzwords. Clearly, we have failed to understand what the word 'feminism' truly means.

'Considering the striated nature of Indian society, it is difficult to comment on the struggles that someone else is having. That's what intersectionality is about. The best I can personally do is to truthfully speak of my own story in my own voice, and support those who attempt to do the same,' says Aditi. 'Feminism has the stereotypes and clichés; the hysterical, the bitch, the anti-men brigade. I don't care. Feminism is ultimately about the equality of access and equal opportunities. And that sounds like the kind of world that would be better for everyone to live in. Why wouldn't we all want that?'

She continues: 'The resistance to feminism and its ideas is confusing to me. But it's probably because it's a call for change. There has to be a change when there is a shift in privilege and power. The person ceding the power is going to feel the pinch. But discomfort is not oppression. Just because XYZ's privilege is being impinged upon, does not mean they are being discriminated against or oppressed.'

We, of course, must be prepared to face some resistance from men, who are going to give up some of their power in the shift. In intimate relationships (father, brother, partner, husband), according to Aditi, we need to 'negotiate and find middle ground' where both parties give up a little of their terrain. But no matter how difficult and awkward they are, we have to have these conversations. Keeping quiet has got us here, and here is not great, so it's time to have these conversations.'

While she honours the disembodiment of the quotidian and of female sexuality, she believes that we cannot alienate men from the process of equality.

'The very thing that tells women that they can't get out of the house at night, also tells men that they cannot cry. Men should be allowed to be as emotional as they want, they should not have the pressure of being the provider in the family. These clichés and stereotypes are what feminists are fighting. Feminism works for men and women. We should all be on board with it,' asserts Aditi.

Aditi further expounds on feminism as she speaks about female bonding and the need for women to 'stand up for the sisterhood'. 'I believe there is a need for conversation even among feminists. Of all shapes, sizes, colours and even genders. We are all aiming for the same thing. The world is a diverse place and everyone has different needs. It will be scary and confusing at times. But what's the point of living in the most democratic age of information in human history, when we are not striving to include every single voice that's able to reach us? Yes, it will be scary and confusing, and mistakes will be made . . . the key is to acknowledge them and to try and fix them.'

Aditi is also vehemently opposed to 'an ideal of a woman'—she doesn't plan to embody or mould anything of the sort. She speaks about how men stare at women, in order to make them feel uncomfortable, and that the whole pressure on women to be feminine is insignificant.

'I am not here to please men. I'm not here to fit into your stereotype of what is acceptable. Women need to be their "filthy, unfeminine self" without being apologetic about it.'

The digital space is one such space that has, in its own way, allowed women to be themselves and engage in dialogue. It is, when used correctly, empowering for women. But it's also come under the heavy hand of fundamentalism, of censorship, draconian restriction, polarization, increasing intolerance across India and an almost hegemonic rule of the state. A woman with an opinion is an easy target, especially in today's saffron environment.

I think of Neeti Palta, another noted comedian, who said: 'It is something to think about, when we become a society where a comedian is afraid to tell a joke, or an artist is afraid to draw a cartoon, but a rapist is not afraid to rape.'[1]

Never have truer words been spoken.

Aditi is, in a similar vein, one of India's most followed but also trolled women on Twitter. How does she cope with threats of rape, acid attack, incarceration, as well as vitriolic remarks about her body and face?

---

[1]   http://www.youthkiawaaz.com/2015/07/neeti-palta-exclusive-interview/" \t "_blank

'The first time I faced a mass exodus of people abusing me, I cried. They asked me how many dicks I had to suck to get into comedy. The funny thing is that when I started my comedy career, there were no "seniors" whose dicks I could suck, so I had a dick-sucking-less entry into comedy.' We laugh. Not the most nuanced statement, but it drives home a point. She continues, 'The first few times I was distraught, but then I realized that it's never going to stop. The appallingly simple solution is to just stand your ground, know that you belong, and make sure they don't silence you. Right now, you must make sure they don't silence you.'

Silenced, she wasn't. Aditi, at the time this book went to press, had almost 389,000 followers on Twitter. That is some critical mass.

'Still, I have no political affiliations. I make fun of whoever is in power,' she says, adding that, 'You have to think of the Internet like an engineering college: it's mostly male. And therefore, as women, we need to stand there and speak. We need to make our voice heard. We need to claim that space: that I am here and I want to be heard. Claim the space that you want to claim.'

Aditi has clearly claimed that space, as she earnestly adds, 'I'm very serious about the way I do comedy because there's a double onus on me as a woman from comedy. I'm very dedicated to it and I try to work harder than others to keep constantly earning my place.'

It has not been easy, but Aditi Mittal is flying the feminist flag high, and making us all laugh while she's at it.

Tanmay Bhat

Founder, All India Bakchod

Stereotypes are not new to Tanmay Bhat. He grew up in hiding because people took a dig at him. He would be upset for days dealing with people making fun of his weight. It wasn't about his talent, his academics, but society just talked way too much about his size.

As a child he had to face unkind body shaming comments, which were devastating at that age. The comparisons, the criticism and confidence-threatening conversations—all would break his resolve to not let his weight issues have an impact on him. 'I think a large part of who I am today as a person has been due to the lingering insecurity I felt about my body since I was a child.'

His mom could observe this and would later recollect in an interview with the *Economic Times*: 'He used to get hurt when people used to tease him, compare him with his cousins. I taught him to build skills that would make people like him, see beyond his weight. He always liked having people around him, so he'd gather people around and tell them jokes; and it worked.'

Three decades later, Tanmay Bhat picked comedy to question stereotypical behaviour and shaming of any kind. To shatter beliefs that suggest women are inferior to men. To influence people about gender equality and feminism.

* * *

Tanmay grew up in a small middle-class family amongst engineers and doctors. He attended Sheth Chunilal Damodardas Barfivala High School, Andheri West. 'In that sense, I am an out and out Mumbai boy.' Tanmay always wanted to be a marine engineer. He loved the high seas and aspired to a life exploring on water, fixing some oil vessel.

But the dream to be went out of the window when one day his parents bought him a cycle. In a post on Humans of Bombay, Tanmay said, 'My parents were concerned with my weight for health reasons, so when I was in Class VIII they bought me a cycle at home and motivated me to lose 5 kg in 6 months. That was a significant incident in my life because even though I had no pressure from my parents, it was an admission of a huge flaw. I remember cycling and weeping because that's when I thought if I couldn't even lose 5 kg, what was I really capable of?'

This changed him. It also challenged his capability. 'From your biggest adversity comes the biggest opportunity.' Tanmay took it upon himself to prove everyone wrong. He says he was never the same again. 'I worked my ass off, my numbers were perfect, I topped my school and my college and became obsessed with making something of myself and proving a point.' And he did. With comedy. But it took him some time to recognize that being a comic was really his calling.

He first noticed his comedy reflexes when he was in Class VII. It started in his building, when there was some function. In Mumbai, building communities are often very active and plan a calendar of events through the year. He somehow gathered the courage to convince the organizers to hand over the stage to him for five minutes. He made people laugh. And laugh out loud. Tanmay recalls this as the litmus test of his comedy instincts. That's when he recognized using it as his guard against body shaming too. 'I used humour as a self-defence mechanism. I loved being the class clown and liked being referred to as "funny".'

Once convinced that comedy was his weapon, it stayed with Tanmay. He grew up to take criticism head-on. 'So very honestly, when people troll me for being fat on Twitter, I actually reply saying "thank you", because if I wasn't fat, I would have never worked this hard. I say thank you because I have an entire career because of it. I say thank you, because if it wasn't for those jokes, I wouldn't have had that much anger in me to go out there and kill it.'

Having succeeded at humour, Tanmay, by the time he turned eighteen, was convinced marine engineering wasn't his thing and he focused on comedy. 'I have gone to every festival from Malhar, an annual festival organized by St Xavier's College, Mumbai, to everything else, just to perform and get on stage. I have written, performed and have been part of events where I've been the only performer because no one else applied. At eighteen, I'd written for *Mumbai Mirror*, and by the age of twenty-five I had written over fifteen television shows—I worked fucking hard,' Tanmay wrote on Humans of Bombay.

Inspiration for his acts came from all quarters. Tanmay watched a great deal of comedy growing up. He idolized Johnny Lever, would mimic and deliver his jokes with ease for hours. His favourite comedian is Russell Peters. Tanmay is inspired by personalities like Raju Shrivastava, Jerry Seinfeld, Chris Rock, George Carlin, Louis CK, and Patrice O'Neal. With all this exposure and passion tucked under his T-shirt, he arrived to do his first stand-up.

'I remember my first legit stand-up happened when Kavi Shastri advised me to talk about who I am. For 20 minutes, I joked about what it's like to be fat and people loved it, and I loved the applause—it was like a drug, like nothing else, and I think that's when I decided I wanted to do this for the rest of my life.'

Having made the choice, Tanmay realizes that with popularity comes responsibility. And just how important comedy can be for breaking stereotypes. It gets the message out. Feminism, through its rise on the front pages, didn't mean too much to Tanmay for a long time. 'Only in the last few years did I understand, appreciate and value the term, and have adopted and identified with it. Outspokenly so. Now, it is a part of my identity and a conscience call to try and leave this planet a little more equal than when I got here.' Tanmay says 'If you believe men and women should have equal rights, that's what makes you a feminist.'

In Tanmay Bhat-style he says, 'Sexism is that final germ left on your body after the Dettol bar gently glides over an animated human anatomy. Feminism is the Dettol detergent that's constantly striving to get rid of that germ.' The quest for a fairer world means you try and keep course, correcting yourself and questioning yourself or just pausing and thinking, 'Is this choice of word/action that I just made, sexist? If yes, how so? And how can I fix it?' You do so knowing that it's hard to forget decades of conditioning.'

Just like comedy, social media has been a transporter of the dialogue in feminism, says Tanmay, whose company is a social media rage and thanks to digital, stand-up comedy is going viral.

Tanmay questions if social media only did it all good. 'Like all things, social media has both contributed and also harmed the movement. On the one hand, it's helped people like me understand the movement in a much more nuanced way, on the other, it's also managed to make feminism a bad word amongst a section of the users.' In some of his videos, he also speaks about the anti-feminism culture becoming a danger to the true form of feminism.

He says, as a result, there are too many definitions we have to contend with. 'The most annoying definition of feminism is "man-hater".'

Tanmay posted a video on Facebook explaining what he thinks about feminism. He says it pains him when people portray feminists as those who constantly whine, '"I am not the feminist type, ya," as if there is a "type",' he questions. 'People say things like real feminists talk about real issues like infanticide and dowry, and not whine about everything,' he says, putting together a sarcastic take on society and how people tag feminists.

He thinks it strange that when people talk about the wage gap or sexism in a movie, these aren't considered 'real issues'. 'What's not a real issue to you is a big issue for others. I don't get women who complain about this stuff. Those who say "I have not faced sexism like that, ya, you are going too much overboard",' Tanmay asserts, such people should not stop others from talking about issues, those who face sexism in and any form and need to voice their issues.

'Equality has been an issue being fought for, for centuries.' Tanmay uses the analogy of the African-American fight against slavery to cite how people on the sidelines become watchers of events. 'I am sure back then there were assholes who were standing on the sidelines and saying "Why these African-Americans are always whining, ya? Why do they always have to crib about this basic equality, ya?" He insists people like that should acknowledge the fact that feminists who talk about 'sexism in movies' and 'wage gap' are not talking superficially and it's an important part of the discussion.

The truth is, Tanmay admits, feminism starts at home. How we are raised, how we treat other women and most importantly, how we recognize that there is a problem that needs to be fixed. 'I find it easiest to be self-deprecatory and call out my own inherent sexism in a funny way, so it becomes easier for others to accept their own flaws. I find it harder to do this on a very wide platform with millions of people, but at a show, it's like a community laughing together, so it's easier to be more vulnerable on stage.'

His mother and female teachers (who formed the majority) had a huge influence on Tanmay being a feminist.

'I once dated a girl who was an outspoken feminist, and she was extremely patient with all my dumb, silly questions. She was extremely well-read and we would often read essays or just discuss for hours at length about different aspects of the feminist movement. There was a very honest understanding between us so it was easier to accept my flaws and problematic behaviour because I was encouraged to improve at every step. I owe so much to the women in my life.'

It's not always simple to convince people around you. Tanmay says WhatsApp jokes are a real reason why stereotypes continue. 'Ignored it for the longest time, until I argued with my aunt who loves forwarding husband–wife jokes. One day, I basically said, "There is not a single wife on this WhatsApp group who is this naggy/dumb/whiny as this joke is trying to portray." Needless to say, that WhatsApp group was quiet for a few days. Until regular programming resumed.'

Perhaps that and everything else he read in the headlines that reeked of stereotypical behaviour, forced him to put it on the forefront of his comedy. Tanmay's feminist work includes 'Rape—It's Your Fault', a dark satirical piece about victim–blaming, and 'Harassment Through the Ages', a parody song that calls out Bollywood's patriarchal nature.

Despite being an advocate of feminism, Tanmay says his definitions are questioned every day, mostly by himself. 'The feminist in me is questioned on a daily basis—mostly by myself, I suppose. Sometimes when I get called out for being sexist or misogynistic, it makes me ridiculously defensive and uncomfortable because it reminds me how far the gap between me and my ideal self still is.' Everybody is learning and growing and the only thing he says he can promise: 'I'll constantly keep trying to be better.'

Tanmay admits he messes up a lot, but learns along the way. 'Right from the writing to the casting. I wouldn't say we're perfect yet, but we're definitely trying. For example, I'm working on balancing the gender ratio in my office. I recognize that it's a male–dominated office, and now I'm actively trying to hire more women in every department to bring us close to equal representation.' He says it can be a challenge sometimes since the idea is not to hire anybody just because of their gender. 'I've made some mistakes in the past, and constant introspection is the only way to try and make the workplace better for women. We are trying to make sure we have equal representation of both genders in the content we produce as well.'

Tanmay says having regret and apology is a big part of who he is, because it makes him a strong man, one who's willing to stand up for a cause and at the same admit when mistakes are made. 'I think for a man, strength is in being vulnerable enough to accept your own mistakes, and continuously striving to live up to the promise of trying to make the world a fairer place for both genders. These are easier said than done because patriarchy runs very, very deep.'

What Tanmay says as we wrap our interview is simple but significant. 'Feminism is about the equality of both genders, but that is achieved by default via the upliftment of women. For all those who ask "why can't we call it equalism or humanism instead of feminism?" Because it's okay to name a movement after the oppressed.'

Deepa Malik

Paralympian

Since the advent of Adam and Eve, Brahma and Vishnu, the Pleistocene Epoch, or whatever human origins you believe in, women have been raised to believe that we are the 'weaker' sex because we are biologically weaker. Anthropologists swear by the comfortable tale that men hunted while women nested, because women were at the mercy of their smaller bodies. After women's lib, these gender constructs were downshifted with claims of women being the 'physically weaker sex' since they were not as strong as men. For aeons we've been given these semantic, biological and evolutionary justifications to mansplain how brute force leaves women vulnerable.

By 2016, India could no longer reduce a woman to her biological abilities because, for the first time in our history, a woman—Deepa Malik—won a medal at the Paralympics. From her wheelchair, she debunked the self-defeating misogynistic myths that her 586 million countrywomen have had to endure. When I read about her triumph, like any curious journalist, I decided that I must interview this fascinating woman. A few weeks later, I found myself entering a five-star hotel room that she was staying in. I was immediately ensconced in Deepa's warmth and friendship. She plied me with wisdom and curated pastries that the chef had specially prepared for her.

It was only when I was on my way back home a few hours later that I realized I hadn't even noticed that she was in a wheelchair. This Panglossian ambience is peculiar to Deepa and also in direct conflict to her life, which would have broken the spirit of a less hardy person.

Deepa was diagnosed with a tumour at an age when most children can't even spell the word 'six'. Her first surgery was at the age of seven. After the cyst was removed, alleviating the pressure on her spinal cord, Deepa spent two years in rehab and learnt how to walk again.

'I've always been a unique idiot,' Deepa laughs when I ask her about this painful period. 'I'm one in ten million, as the doctor told me. But I had defiance. I had the DNA of an outdoorsy child. So, the minute I could walk again, I ran out to play. I loved riding the tricycle with my older brother, or playing cricket with boys.' At a time when sports were considered a boy's domain and indoor games a girl's domain, Deepa broke stereotypes and played outdoor sports. 'I was lucky to have a progressive father who never stopped me from playing "boy" games.'

Her activities didn't stop at home. During her time at Kendriya Vidyalaya—a school run by the Central government—and at Sophia Girls' College in Ajmer, Deepa played basketball, kabaddi and cricket.

Her activities didn't stop when she got married at the age of twenty. 'My husband, Colonel Bikram Singh, knew that I was interested in biking, so he gifted me a bike. Therefore, within two years I got married, became a biker and had a child.' But tragedy struck again, and this time it afflicted her daughter, Devika. 'I was only twenty-two when my daughter got into an accident. After my own childhood trauma, I had to train my daughter to begin walking again. It was tough.'

Deepa still kept up her spirits and decided to have another baby. A second daughter was born to her and she named her Ambika, goddess of the moon. This was in 1995.

In 1999, a doctor diagnosed Deepa with spastic paraplegia and told her that she had seven days before she became a paraplegic. At the age of twenty-nine, Deepa was sentenced to a lifetime in a wheelchair.

To go from being a healthy, active woman to being told that a cyst in her spinal cord would leave her paralysed from the chest down, Deepa was left devastated. In a few days she would undergo two spinal surgeries, resulting in hundreds of stitches between her shoulder blades. To add to her woes, Deepa's husband was serving in Kargil and she had two young daughters—aged eight and four—at home. For six days, Deepa stayed in bed and wrote a lot of—in her own words—'sullen' poetry.

'Although the poetry was good, it was sad. It showed me how depressed and under-confident I was feeling. I realized that I needed to change. That's when I started writing about dreams and success. That's when the real transformation happened within me. You don't have to wait for change to happen to you. You have to become the change.'

So when informed that she had two options in front of her: to call her parents who lived in Jaipur to come and take care of her, or to call her husband back home, Deepa decided to take neither.

'I didn't consider either of them an option,' Deepa recalls. 'As far as I knew, this was my problem and I was determined not to let it affect my family or me. Whatever else I did, I never wanted to become dependent on them or anyone else.'

She could've watched all the branches on a fig tree die, in true Sylvia Plath style, but instead Deepa went about doing what she's best at: being proactive. She got her house wheelchair-friendly. She equipped her house with a surgical bed and a wooden ramp. She installed remote bells for her neighbours, so she could reach them in case of an emergency. She took away crystal decorations, and put away her expensive clothes and jewellery. She hired help that was more than part-time. 'I had to do all this with limited financial support,' she confesses.

Instead of breaking her body, mind and spirit, as disability is wont to do, Deepa says it brought her life into focus. 'After my surgeries, I went through strenuous rehab for around three years. I had to go to the hospital therapy room every single day where a physiotherapist and doctor made me exercise, and taught me how to move my body from, say, one chair to another, or from a bed to a chair. In 2002, I moved into a farmhouse with my in-laws. There, I had access to neither friends nor a regular life, like going out for a movie or to the club. To pass my time, I opened a home-delivery service that later turned into a lucrative garden restaurant. It was here that I made many friends among college kids and young army officers. I started rehabilitating boys who were working with me, and provided them with education and vocational training. These boys became my family. I also bought myself a specialized bike from Kaulson Racing.' As a result, Deepa would take her custom-made motorcycle for a spin every Sunday. 'Those were good times.'

But fate was not finished with Deepa. Seven years after her diagnosis, in 2006, at the age of thirty-six, Deepa got another shock. The doctors told her that only her arms would remain functional and she would have a little strength left in her neck. That was all that would be left of her once able body. Again, Deepa did not cower. Again, she refused to let this dictate the kind of life she might have. She crawled out from under her disability and carried it around like a brick in her pocket. She used that brick to hurl at glass ceilings, shattering many at a time. She wore her lucky charm, a brass bracelet with 'Om Namah Shivai' inscribed on it, which she'd picked up from a temple in Ranikhet, and decided to become an adrenalin junkie; the complete opposite of her diagnosis.

Through online research she realized that the best rehab for her was in water. 'So, I put on a swimming costume and refused to feel embarrassed. Swimming was part of my recovery. Within seven days, I was swimming using only my arms and shoulders. I didn't stop at that. Soon I was swimming competitively. I started winning medals internationally, but not nationally. I made the Limca record (*Limca Book of Records*) in 2008 for swimming upstream across the Yamuna,' Deepa says.

'I had to leave swimming due to the infrastructure challenges in India. There were no heated pools available to practise, even during winter months, and my body could not swim in such cold water. But I didn't slow down. When I could no longer be a swimmer, I became a car rally driver,' Deepa recalls.

She tells me that her financial emancipation helped her. She got a specialized gadget put in her car, procured her licence with some difficulty, and started driving. Soon, Deepa was the first person in India to receive a licence for a modified rally vehicle. Subsequently, she became a navigator and driver in the Raid-de-Himalaya 2009 and Desert Storm 2010. In 2011, she drove across nine high-altitude passes in nine days on India's highest motorable road in Ladakh. And, in 2013, she drove the entire length from Chennai to Delhi.

'I became a newsmaker after riding a special bike on *MTV Roadies* S05,' Deepa laughs on whipping up the memory.

It was around this time that Deepa decided to also become . . . an athlete. She explained this rationale: 'When I exercised, people would say, "She's doing physio for her recovery." But when I played sports, they'd call me a *khiladi*. I liked that. I also began to enjoy the physical fitness routine as a sportsperson. So I decided to pursue it.'

Deepa began training in Paralympic sports like javelin, shot-put and discus throw. 'My only other option as a para athlete was wheelchair racing that I didn't have the money to pursue. Seated throws were also the best for my body.'

In order to prepare for that, she had to close down her beloved restaurant after running it for seven years, and move from Ahmednagar to Delhi, as it had better sports facilities. In a field where people began training from the time they were teenagers, Deepa was two decades too late: she was thirty-six years old. Her training schedule for the Paralympics was gruelling. Deepa would drive her specially modified SUV from Gurgaon to the Siri Fort Sports Complex, where she would train for three hours, return home, and then practise for three hours again in the evening.

'I took a lot of help from bikers and rally people to assist me. They truly facilitated my sports journey. I took neither a penny from my house nor help from any household member. No offence towards my husband,' she adds, 'but he followed a stereotypical path of looking after a paraplegic. He limited me in his head because he thought that would make me comfortable. But when I broke those stereotypes, he didn't stop me. He told me to pursue sports but was honest that he could not afford the expensive equipment. He couldn't even offer surrogate support since he'd left the army, because of which I didn't get accommodation wherever I went to train. Ever since I started my sports journey, I have not taken a single penny from my husband. The fact that I am not a single mother takes away from my journey of living like a single mother.'

No sportswoman in India has had it easy. I've interviewed gymnast Dipa Karmakar in Agartala and one of her biggest battles was the access to facilities in a remote part of India. Wrestler Sakshi Malik's greatest battle was patriarchy in her village. Boxer Mary Kom's, in her own way, was motherhood. Deepa's battles were much more than mental or external. Her quest was to conquer the body that had conquered her.

She trained from morning till night. When she trained, she got spasms. She had to time every minute, from the moment she woke up till she slept. Her meals had to be carefully timed. In the absence of any control over her body temperature, bladder and bowel movements, she measured and watched 'every drop of water and food' that she consumed. While training, she would eat six eggs and half a kilogram of lean meat every day. Four months before a competition, she would stop eating carbohydrates and sugar. Since she had no stomach muscles, Deepa had to painstakingly manage her bladder and bowel movements. Despite this litany of struggles, Deepa continued to smile.

'I knew that somehow or the other, I would push my body to the absolute limit. Because I knew that winners don't do things differently, they do different things. By being a differently-able person, everything I did was different,' she said.

From this cauldron of fragmented hopes, Deepa created something magical. She took part in the 2010 Commonwealth Games, where she eventually finished sixth in her category in the shot-put. Her first big win came when she won a bronze at the Asian Games in 2010. Instead of resting on her laurels, Deepa wanted her wins to carry meaning.

'There were prejudices I faced as a para sportswoman, so I wanted to use my medal to support women with disabilities in India. This was when I joined camp in the Sports Authority of India, and realized the disparity between paraplegics and the able-bodied. Para athletes would be given Rs 1 lakh for the same win that an able-bodied sportsman would be given Rs 10 lakh. That's when I became a sports activist. I started fighting for us.'

With that came some more rigours. 'From July 2012 to 2014, I faced the biggest challenges of my life. I didn't have a restaurant, a job or government grants, but my expenses were huge. My coach also sabotaged me. I still wanted to be a Paralympian. I didn't want to be defeated. I continued training. To earn money, I became a motivational speaker. Fortunately, I got a government salary in 2014, which helped me focus on that year's Asian Games and win a medal.'

Deepa's journey outside the sports field was not easy either. As history has long witnessed, there is a huge tendency of self-flagellation with women. After motherhood, most women become stay-at-home parents or return to a less engaging professional job. The ones who become working women, say that it often takes almost nothing at all for society to censure and criticize them. If they miss a PTA meeting because of an office deadline or seek respite in a movie, their neighbours and acquaintances immediately accuse them of being 'neglectful' or 'bad mothers'. No wonder it is said that 'show me a woman without guilt and I'll show you a man'. Deepa faced similar mother-shaming attitudes. 'Once I bought Milano biscuits for Devika since Hrithik Roshan was advertising them. When she went to school with these, a teacher told her, "Your mother is bringing you up on biscuits."' But Deepa decided not to pander to these outdated notions. 'These attitudes need to stop,' she decided. 'I ignored the immediate voices around me. Instead I would look at my daughters' faces and know that I was doing a good job. The right question we need to ask ourselves is not "can I have it all?", but "can I have what's important for my family and me?" When the mothers didn't invite me to picnics or movies, I created a restaurant. When they didn't take me anywhere because of my chair, I showed them where my chair can take me.'

As Gloria Steinem said, 'It's not about biology but about consciousness.'

In Jawaharlal Nehru's book *Letters from a Father to His Daughter* (dedicated to Indira Gandhi), he said that we must learn to step outside our own boundaries to understand the world. Deepa felt the same.

'I was not an ordinary mother. I was exposed to a lot,' she adds. Her daughters would take turns to accompany their mother on her sports tournaments. 'Travelling with me provided interested learning for them. It gave them exposure to different platforms. From not having any money to travelling abroad, staying in five-star hotels, to rubbing shoulders with inspirational people, they've seen it all. One day they would be biking alongside John Abraham, the next day they would attend a fun college event with stand-up shows and pop music. I've made the journey fun by not being a disabled mother, but by being a fun-loving, active and adventurous mother who has given them a healthy and positive attitude to life. I have connected with them by staying young at heart. I've raised them as free women. I've taught them how to be safe, but never restricted them. They've grown up to be very sensitive girls. They love staying with me, not to take care of me, but so that I can take care of them! We really need to create an atmosphere where women can reach out and excel. We need to give our young girls an opportunity to do that.'

She shouldered on. Then: at the age of forty-six, despite being the oldest member of our country's Paralympic Games team (in addition to suffering from a neck injury), Deepa created history and became the only woman from India to win a medal at the Paralympic Games.

World championships are extremely important to a country like ours, especially given the apathetic treatment of sportswomen in our country. With these wins, Deepa has become the torchbearer for both women and the disabled. For instance, while there is widespread awareness about the Olympics and others sporting events, Paralympics was brought into the limelight with Deepa's win. While her win meant a lot for special sporting events, there is still little conversation about the disabled in our society.

Deepa insists that the disabled can achieve their goals if they have a dauntless spirit to pursue a passion. 'There is an urgent need to dispel the taboos and myths associated with physically challenged people. Both the government and society should come forward to create facilities for them.'

Her win has also made a strong statement for older sportspeople. Deepa was in her forties when she had her biggest win, even though sportspeople are said to peak in their mid-twenties. Despite becoming a sportsperson in her mid-thirties, she's won fifty-eight national and state-level gold, and eighteen international medals, holds four records in the *Limca Book of Records*, one Arjuna award and one Padma Shri Award.

Deepa has shown us how powerful the female body can be. She has shown us that it is the mind that conquers the body and not patriarchy. This notion extends beyond pure physical strength. We need more ideas of sexuality, beauty and the female body. We need to break free from the internalized male gaze. We must decide how we want to be represented. While commenting on representation, we must be careful not to shame sex and the body. More than anything else, women need to stop being critical of other women's bodies, and, more importantly, of their own bodies. This will mean truly disempowering the deeply entrenched notions of misogyny.

Deepa also champions the idea of India taking the lead in gender equality. 'To achieve the dream of an accessible and inclusive India, it is important to provide its women and differently-abled with equal opportunities,' she says. 'Instead of restricting them within the four walls of their houses, they should be provided with opportunities and the freedom to chase their dreams. Instead of asking them to stay at home, we must create a safer and more respectful environment for them. This is important. The growth of a nation can be measured by how its women and differently-abled people are treated.'

Deepa's voice echoes that idea that sometimes, it's not about accolades but about empowerment.

'Life is a festival that should be celebrated every day, and to celebrate it, we should have some credos, goals, and objectives that bring value addition in our life and society as a whole. We should assign jobs and responsibilities to employees as per their calibre and capacities.'

I agree. I didn't realize just how tough life gets for Deepa because she is not the kind of person who will admit it, but when I invited her for a women's conference in Delhi, the organizers booked her a Toyota Innova instead of a Tata Indigo. I greeted her at the hotel lobby only to be mortified as she struggled to get out of the car. It didn't daunt her spirit, of course, she spoke to a standing ovation, giving me—the moderator—and our audience goose bumps, but I also understood then why she calls for a collective responsibility.

'Society needs to break taboos around disabilities and create an inclusive space,' Deepa tells me. 'Instead of questioning our capabilities and creating stereotypes, people must try and remove the taboos and myths around disability and give us an opportunity, give us a chance. Create facilities where we can go and exercise our hobbies.'

Today, thanks to the efforts and struggles of paralympians like Deepa, there have been many positive changes for para sportspeople. 'Today, the policies are in place,' Deepa tells me. 'We have an office, infrastructure, exposure, media, and a more educated and inclusive approach. An academy is being made for us. Even our funding has increased.'

'Earlier I wouldn't get Rs 5,000, but now I get Rs 5 lakhs for a one-hour talk. I have a bigger bank balance, a bigger house, and I'm finally in the tax bracket. I'm even learning the nuances of GST (goods and services tax)!'

She adds that her friends, many of them ladies over the age of forty, have begun new careers and started new hobbies, using Deepa as a benchmark. 'Earlier, people felt sorry for me, now some of them are jealous of me.' She laughs, with her big throaty laugh that is as big and welcoming as her accomplishments. 'This is good. It makes me feel human.'

Despite the jokes and bonhomie, she takes her newfound status as a role model very seriously. 'Heavy is the head that wears the crown. You have a lot of responsibilities. You can't be careless. You become a more aware citizen and more positive. The best part is that you become an inspiration to good initiatives like the Swachh Bharat Abhiyan (a government mission for a clean India) and the Beti Bachao, Beti Padhao Yojana (a government mission to save and educate the girl child). The worst part is that people think that you know everything about every subject—from politics to maths. I am expected to give a statement on anything that's happening in the country! Life is also difficult in terms of time management. I have so much work that I can't train! But . . . I'm loving it!'

From times before and after Darwin, who received credit for the theory of evolution instead of his peer Alfred Russel Wallace, names are lost in the shuffle of time. No wonder then that history is said to be a tale written by men such that women are rarely seen in it. But Deepa has rewritten history. She's defeated her disability using not just physical strength but an unbelievable amount of mental strength. She has been inspirational to our nation, to our disabled and to our women. She has taken disability and given it ability.

Being disabled was Deepa's most visible identity, but she refused to make it her most defining identity. We can't help but salute her.

Malishka Mendonsa

Radio Jockey

The morning Malishka Mendonsa woke up in New York, she couldn't have imagined that a parody she sang would have caught the entire country's imagination. Suddenly from being a crib on radio and YouTube, it had become a national obsession. This was a satirical song targeting the municipal corporation for the potholes on the roads and other civic issues that the people of Mumbai generally faced. The Shiv Sena, which controls the municipal corporation of Mumbai, better known as the BMC, criticized Malishka publicly. The song had gone viral.

Malishka didn't take it lying down. She hit back at the civic body in a cheeky way, saying she was ready with six more songs. She wrote, 'I am a rapper now. Also a breeder apparently.' Social media, news channels, and newspapers supported her. And that breeder bit? BMC had sent her and her mom a notice for allegedly breeding dengue mosquitoes in their flat at Bandra. They were obviously short of ideas of accusing her in a 'legal' way.

Malishka hadn't come to virtual blows like this ever before. She says she was very scared. 'It was all so new to me,' she recalls. 'I was very vulnerable and angry. I felt all sorts of things to begin with. I did get scared a bit. Being a strong woman sometimes can bother you because you are constantly telling yourself you are a rock star.'

But what were the options? She simply took them on. She didn't cow down in fear (on the face of it). She didn't let others take her down. She stood up for herself. 'It's who I am. I grew up with a strong mother,' she says in answer to what makes her a feminist. 'For me, I think everything must be about feminism. It's about not breaking anyone's rights and spaces. It's true for both men and women. Can we treat each other as human kind?'

Malishka talks about the need for women to speak up because it can spark a movement. 'Speaking up is not a publicity stunt,' she says reflecting on the #MeToo campaign which triggered women across the world to talk about harassment and assault. This was in the aftermath of a series of exposés involving Harvey Weinstein who had sexually exploited women he worked with in Hollywood, abusing his position of power as a mega film producer. 'It's important and thanks to social media, it's good that we can make our voices felt and heard. It's a vocalization. Every woman will put her hand up when I ask how many have a #MeToo story. Why can't women make a noise and tell you what they go through?' Malishka contends it is important for men to realize that half the population must have a voice. And that some stuff may make them uncomfortable. 'We have become a nation of hypocrites. We have heard of the Kamasutra and Khajuraho and then we say sex is a taboo topic. All this rubbish we hear. There is so much pent-up anger in us.'

* * *

Malishka Mendonsa grew up in Mumbai with a single mom. Living in the suburbs of Andheri, she studied at Sophia's (Sophia College for Women) in Breach Candy in the south of the city. Growing up she saw her mom go through a hard middle-class life: paying the bills, balancing a job and raising her daughter and a son. 'My father passed away when I was really young. My mother brought me up entirely. She had to deal with a lot. She was an office-going woman. She faced property issues and other family challenges after my dad's death. Hats off to her gumption.'

Not for just raising her well, but also for raising her to be fearless. That's what Malishka says most about her mom. 'Your confidence is the only thing you need to wear. Whether you are in a workplace, in a relationship, or anything, that's what mom always said to me. You just have to love yourself a great deal and that's immense hard work,' Malishka says. She reminds herself every day: 'You have to say to yourself . . . I am the person who will not take some stuff and you will just not take it. You will be yourself. Just yourself.'

Malishka then joined St. Xavier's College, down the road from the grand Victoria Terminus in Mumbai, to study communications. After two years of being there, with stints in dramatics, she set course to look for a job. The communications market in the late nineties was tough. The media wasn't this established. 'So I simply read *Harry Potter* for three weeks. Just spending my time.'

It didn't bother her that she hadn't yet got a job. She always felt things would eventually work out. 'I have been taking risks. I was always a *nautanki*. I used to do this with mohalla students—singing, dancing and practising Bollywood numbers. I won a prize when I was in the sixth standard. I always wanted to dance and perform and be on stage. You know me as a radio person. But I was a total dramatics person. I joined everything in Xavier's when I moved there. You should be able to do everything. Why should people box you? Stay unboxed.'

She was gifted with a heavy, full voice, but during college, it didn't go beyond the family audiences in the auditorium or announcements during the farewells. Her friends asked her to experiment with her voice. 'I finally thought I would give it a try.' She started getting voice-over assignments. 'I got voice-over assignments from Discovery and CNN, big names those days in India.' Little did she know, in three weeks, she would be hosting on radio. 'That was it. There was no looking back. Eighteen years of doing radio, and here I am.' Over the years, this relentless love of radio earned her the moniker Mumbai ki Rani, RJ Malishka.

What really broke the ice with the listeners was her ability to go beyond belting out top of the pops. She didn't look down upon her listeners, she heard them out. Spoke to them about everyday issues. Earlier through emails, postcards, and of late, through social media. That audience connection is what also empowers her to push boundaries. By her own admission, she is known as the 'ballsy' one among her colleagues.

'That's how I was while growing up, too. I felt the need to experiment. When you are younger, try out as much as you can. Sometimes you can be a hostess. Wear a sari and be one. You should try. It gets harder as you grow up. But while you can, it allows you to explore other things and yourself. And that's why, even now, even today, I push boundaries. I think it's in my spirit to experiment that clicks well with my listeners.'

Growing up, Malishka's mom may have protected them from patriarchal mindsets but society did the opposite.

Somewhere between junior college and communications, Malishka put on a lot of weight. Her size never bothered her. 'Because it wasn't part of my existence and my job. But I would be lying if I say it wouldn't affect me, when my mom came after me.' She says it was not about the looks and her weight didn't interfere with jobs she had. 'Never, ever,' she emphasizes. 'I'm so much more than my weight. I am an RJ who will speak her mind.'

Malishka did a variety of physical workouts to get back in shape. She followed a rigorous routine of dance, Pilates, yoga, running and lost more than 15 kg in almost five months. 'I used to work out for two-and-a-half hours at a stretch.'

It started with a cardio-elliptical trainer, cycling and weights and soon she was doing mixed martial arts.

Then diets, which she found hard to stick to, she admits. 'I would be on-air till 11 a.m., after which I would go for my Pilates classes. Then I would come back to the office, work on the next day's show, and head to the gym.'

However, this workout didn't come easy on the mind. People loved her voice but questioned her weight. Their opinions came in sacks full. 'When you're chubby, they will comment. Body shaming comes so easy to us. . . they would casually say, "You're talented but you're fat," and once the weight-loss happened, it was, "You're so gorgeous . . . awww, you've lost so much . . ." This annoys me.'

Malishka wasn't new to judgements. She had seen some growing up. As a child, the mothers of her mom's generation were fiercely protective. But of their sons. 'They used to raise them calling them breadwinners. And I would be forever amused. Even if it were a laddoo, the moms would want their son to get it, not their daughters.' Given her own liberal upbringing, she would ask her mom. 'How many homes in our country have the same issues? He needs more nutrition because he is the boy. He will go to school. These stories really impacted me.'

Malishka says something that sticks with me: Part of feminism is really being true to yourself and your desires. It's also about you coming face to face with your fears. Having time with yourself. The willingness to pay attention to oneself. 'No matter how it manifests. I conquered my love for diving. I was petrified. I started crying. But when you are able to do something like this and you succeed, you realize how important this is.' Women often don't care about what they might love doing. Or they brush it aside for something at work or for the sake of the family. 'I wanted it. I tried it. It was liberating.' She says one must take a chance on oneself. 'When I was in the water, I realized how small I was in that massive ocean. Even that small fish was cooler than me. That wiped my stress out,' she says of the constant sense of over-achievement we all have is from living in a hyper-connected world. Could finding yourself be a feminist resolve? Malishka puts it simply. 'Let chill takeover the *sarvanaash* (mayhem and destruction) feeling.'

But it's after all easier said than done. Most people don't find the courage to go on a soul search. Others don't have the privilege. And so, Malishka says, we need to level the field for women by going that extra mile and giving them a hand. That's the other narrative that bothers Malishka, of how women treat women. Are they judgemental? Didn't Hillary Clinton say there is a special place in hell for women who don't help other women? Malishka says we all carry the responsibility of lifting other women. 'When I am at work, I always make it a point to help another colleague, or a junior. I am conscious about making an effort to given them a pat on the back. To help shape what they most want from work. To build that other person. Our traditions, unfortunately, haven't really taught us that and so it's a process of unlearning and learning.'

Has media chronicled more of gossipy women who can't stand each other, and has that fed our sensibilities for the most time? 'It is so difficult for the media to believe that three women can have fun without having to bitch about each other. I think there is a bit too much we make about this issue. Women, too, take women up just as much as men do for men. There are so many stories of women helping women's empowerment and that's the narrative I choose to push forward.'

Malishka debuted in the film *Tumhari Sulu,* in which Vidya Balan enacts the part of a radio jockey. 'A great example of modern-day feminism is *Tumhari Sulu.* I am going to do my responsibilities, and I will be just fine doing my job and having love for my relationship.' Malishka insists that feminism needs to be re-understood as something that's every day and a part of our life. 'Feminist has become a *gaali* (abuse). People need some education. We need a re-understanding. I am a feminist because I choose not to do house work? Isn't that just a lazy and random definition? For me, feminism is a natural state of mind. It's not a surprise, or some *chaunka dene wala* concept.'

It's one thing to be a strong woman. It's quite another to be a strong woman standing up and speaking for all. 'I have used my position of influence with grace to be a strong woman. I have heard whispers about myself: "Arré, she is a strong woman," but that's good for me. I am proud and happy to say I have managed. You can wake me up and ask me to speak on film, feminism, molestation, and I would. Apart from getting trolled on my time for speaking my mind, I think I have ensured people sit up and take notice when I opine.' Of course, at times she is criticized for being a woman with a voice.

'Although, for myself, I have not carved a differentiation but I see it coming at me beyond my life in radio. Since I am now venturing out, I was just having this conversation with some people in television. There, we do see some body shaming. Men are the lead characters. Women characters are either Sati Savitri or ambitious demons, as if they are nothing in between. It's quite problematic that either you are deified or objectified. Women just touch the feet of elders and make samosas, c'mon let's get beyond it.'

Malishka asserts that the notion of feminism is so convoluted in India that if you seek your freedom and rights, people question your seeking women's seats in a bus. As though the two should be equated. 'I feel like telling people that the day they start keeping their hands to themselves, women would stop seeking reserved chairs.'

Through her radio show, Malishka has put her life journey—one that's far from easy—out there. She has put all thoughts on things from Bollywood, local trains, to sexual harassment on the streets of Mumbai.

Malishka dropped her second name the day she got on radio. I ask her why. 'I wanted to be a radio jockey. A person for *all*. I wanted to speak in people's own language. Like in Mumbai, speak Marathi. I felt that the second name attached identities sometimes. I didn't want to be told that, "Oh, she is Catholic and she is talking like that, how cool." I wanted it to be normal.' Then she quickly adds that it was a bad move in hindsight. 'I wish I hadn't dropped my first name . . . because my first name has become RJ and my second name Malishka!!' she laughs.

Malishka has been the quintessential Mumbai girl for years. 'Everything you can give your kids, yourself, you have to just go with your guts. Be your own favourite person.'

Gul Panag

Actor, Politician, Entrepreneur

In 1999, when Gul Panag was crowned Miss India, my family acquired bragging rights. Our grandparents were neighbours in Chandigarh; we shared a compound wall and a mango tree. Such small coincidences made us proud, and precocious. That summer I happened to be on vacation in Chandigarh. In the leafy by-lanes of Sector 11, there was not much to do except drink tall glasses of mango lassi and stave off boys on their *geri* route. So, my cousins and I would peer over the compound wall and stick our heads through the grills of the front gate, hoping to catch a glimpse of the beauty queen. We never did.

Later that year, we huddled together to watch Gul at the Miss Universe pageant. My beloved Nani cooed when she saw Gul on TV. 'Look at her. And look at you,' she said, glaring at my oversized spectacles and unflattering bangs. 'You should get your head out of books and see what women are accomplishing nowadays.' But it wasn't Gul's beauty and poise that struck me that day; it was her eloquent answer. When Jack Wagner asked her what Miss Mexico and she had debated, she replied: 'What we did debate was the position of women and how the social revolution, which has overtaken Mexico, has really improved the position of women. We debated about whether the revolution occurred earlier in India or in Mexico. I conceded defeat.'

As a teenager growing up in relatively safe Mumbai, I'd never really thought about the position of women before. But I sat there, with my Nani—who had never entered a school but who, after becoming a widow at the age of thirty-five, scraped together whatever little money she had to send her four daughters to Shimla's best schools—and realized an epic truth. My uneducated grandmother may not have experienced much outside the role of a daughter, wife and mother, yet she innately knew what women could achieve. I understood then that sometimes we don't need a revolution to improve the lives of women. We need just one woman to care about the position of other women. Gul had hit home.

As the next few years took me abroad for my studies and job, I came upon news about Gul from online portals and my family. She had joined films, I was told. This was not unexpected. She was a talented actor doing offbeat, thought-provoking films, To me, this was also not unexpected. Without even knowing her, I could never imagine Gul as the quintessential beauty pageant winner. I always imagined her as more than the sum of her parts. So, on a snowy day in Switzerland, when a friend brought a DVD of a film called *Dor*, I was not surprised to see Gul featured in it. After all, the film was about female friendship and the duality of tradition versus freedom, which is the bane of most Indian women. It was one of the most evolved cinematic experiences I'd had. The film seemed like an extension of the person that Gul was and what she projected—courage, fearlessness and evolution. This fact was further evident when she acted in other equally evocative films like *Dhoop* and *Manorama Six Feet Under*.

In the misogynistic world of Bollywood, Gul was not going to play second-fiddle to her male counterparts. She was going to be neither a sidekick nor a scorekeeper. She was going to be treated on the basis of her merit and talent, and not her beauty and gender. In a world that relegated women by representing them in two ways—as conniving and horny krantikaaris, or insipid and vanilla *abla naris*, Gul was going to be neither. She was going to make wiggle room for the normal, educated, intelligent and smart woman.

Once again, I was proud.

Many years later, I returned to India when my second book was published. The India I returned to had changed out of sight. The population growth, the spread of social media, and the immediacy of news had shape-shifted the country to one that I was taking time to reacquaint with. More importantly, the presence of women in it felt so much more immediate . . . and boisterous. Their outrage no longer existed only in pockets. Their thoughts did not live quietly in the shadow of great events. I was excited about this, also scared. My books were exploring the human cost of these changes.

This was the time that I finally got to meet Gul. We were both invited to the Chandigarh Literature Festival, and happened to be speakers on the same panel. What immediately struck me about Gul was her humility, down-to-earthness, intelligence and wit. She was the person she embodied in public life. This was refreshing. Traits like these are rare in someone so accomplished, so young. With her I felt no point wasting time in niceties; I got straight down to brass tacks.

'What is familiar does not have to be what is good,' I remember discussing with her.

'Many people don't know this about me but I was due to start studying at Kellogg School of Management after I became Miss India. On the eve of my departure, I changed my mind. I realized that after Kellogg, I would be just another cog in the wheel. But being an actor would open up a lot of doors for me. And I wanted more doors. Public life was the endgame for me, for which I wanted gravitas. My choice of cinema was dictated by this future I had in mind for myself. Therefore, acting for me became a means to an end, not the end itself,' she said. 'This is why I consider someone like Shabana Azmi my role model.'

Interestingly that journey towards public life began with Gul observing India's changes at the experiential level . . . through her travels as the intrepid woman traveller. In a country where a woman is raped every twenty minutes and many women do not venture out of their homes, Gul travelled to about twenty-four states in India and sixty countries around the world. She wanted to be transported to realms beyond tossing coins in the Trevi Fountain and watching a Broadway show at Times Square.

'My father was in the army so I was brought up as a road-trip kid. Twice a year my father would take us for camping trips. Travel is second nature to me. Even after Miss India, travel was on my agenda.'

The key was not to overthink it: 'I would take my jeep or bike and drive cross-country with my boyfriend (now husband) and girlfriends. In fact, in 2002 I took my first biking trip with my boyfriend to Ladakh, where our brothers also later tagged along.' She laughed at the memory.

But there have also been some not-so-laughable incidents. 'Recently my friend Swati Mallik and I went travelling across the north-east of India. We were at Arunachal Pradesh, when Swati, who is an avid photographer, stood on a hairpin bend taking a photograph. A truck carrying ten feet of *sariya* (steel bars) came towards her. I shouted out to warn her and she ducked, but only at the last second.'

Gul's travel lessons are clear: be present, even when you lose yourself in a moment.

'I have mostly had good experiences during my travels. You have to start with the default position that people are there to help you. Locals will be welcoming and friendly if you come across as someone who engages with them and shows interest.'

'I enjoy travelling alone as well,' she added. 'When you're alone, your social commitments are zero, so you can really interact with the local culture and people. You're forced to strike up conversations and blend with locals.'

'The first time I travelled alone was to backpack across Europe when I was a nineteen-year-old student. After that I've done some solo trips overseas and gone on my bike to places like Pondicherry, Srinagar, Ladakh, Ooty and Indore.'

I'd had my share of travels by then—a combination of the mundane and offbeat. Like many Indians, I was seeking adventures to unfamiliar territory that took me outside of myself. I'd cycled down a dormant volcano in Hawaii, gone solo snorkeling in Bali, and enjoyed a champagne breakfast in the middle of the Masai Mara, surrounded by wild and dangerous animals. I'd eaten unusual food like the fugu fish (blowfish) in Japan (more poisonous than cyanide if not properly cooked), the Haggis in Scotland, and fried ostrich balls in Nairobi. I thought of myself as adventurous. But would I possess the same bravado if I had to travel alone across India? No. The truth was, and I realize this now, I would rather risk being poisoned by fugu fish than risk being raped.

Clearly, a woman travelling alone in India is not safe. How then did she do it?

'I took solo trips only to places where I knew the lay of the land or knew people,' Gul replied. 'It's not safe to be a solo traveller, especially if you're a woman. Travelling solo comes with a position of privilege and maturity. If you must, then take calculated risks.' A pause. 'A road trip with two or more girls is more advisable than going alone. Avoid driving if you're a solo traveller, man or woman, since you may experience fatigue issues. Solo biking is different, of course, since you can't really fall asleep during it. Don't drive after dark, as it's harder to deal with curveballs, like a puncture. Make sure your lodging is taken care of beforehand, so you don't waste time or money after reaching your destination. Plan your route far ahead. Be open to spontaneity. Adventure is not being reckless but taking calculated risks and then going with the flow.'

Gul had done it despite the fact that just the previous year she'd been molested at a marathon where she'd gone running.

'Like all Indian women, I've been touched a countless number of times in crowded places; whether it's a bus, a train, a *mela*, or a marathon,' she said. 'These men at the marathon didn't know who I was. I was just another body to them. This emboldened them. In our country people feel they can get away with this behaviour because a woman will turn around and say, "*Kiska haath tha*? (Whose hand was that?)". It is the power of anonymity in a crowd. This attitude comes from a space of objectifying women.'

'But why do people stare at women? Are we a novelty?' she continued. 'An elephant walking on the road is a novelty but we will not stare at it because we have seen elephants. But when a foreigner comes to India he will stare at an elephant because he has never seen something like that on the street. Therefore, if more and more women were partaking in things that everybody does, whether they were traffic cops, policewomen, doctors or lawyers, things would change. If women are more evolved in every field of life, men would get used to the fact that they are around. In the north, we don't see much participation of women in society. Therefore, if they see a woman in an office, where there are two women for every ten men, they'll say, "Oh . . . *kaam karne aai hai* . . . *achha?* (Oh . . . she's working . . . really?)" It's not normal for them to believe that women can work or be independent.'

Instead of allowing the system to dictate how she should behave, Gul possessed the courage to dictate change to the system.

'But, it should be okay for men to see women everywhere. We have to desensitize men from this notion that women are to be seen only occasionally. For example, in Mumbai we see a lot of women on the road and out on the streets, as compared to men. But in the north the ratio is far less. For every X number of men, you will see X over three women. That's why women become a novelty and something to stare at. At some point, women need to be equal stakeholders everywhere, including on the road. We need to put more women out there.'

Meanwhile, Gul took on another adventure: of becoming an entrepreneur. This was a role she considered more important to her than anything else she had undertaken. She co-founded a tech start-up MobieFit (with Gourav Jaswal) that makes fitness apps, like First Run. Why fitness?

'It has nothing to do with vanity,' Gul clarified. 'As urban Indian women, we are trying to do everything and, therefore, we are overworked. I'll go home and want to put up my feet, but I will not because I'll have to take care of a hundred things. From being a professional in the workspace to wanting to be the perfect homemaker, we are striving for everything. The only thing that can help us achieve these goals is to be healthier and get fitter. That was the reason to start this company.'

The company makes many apps for corporate and individual solutions. 'We are the single-largest indigenously developed suite of fitness and health applications in India,' Gul says proudly. 'The USP of our products is that they are voice-coached.'

In 2013, Gul founded another company called Tittar Lodge Productions.

'We make high-quality and cutting-edge lifestyle content focused on travel, adventure and food, for networks like Discovery Channel and platforms like ScoopWhoop and Arré. We also produce content for brands like MakeMyTrip, Mahindra & Mahindra Ltd and Triumph Motorcycles. Brouhaha is our independent and original content vertical that has snack-sized lifestyle content that's the digital answer to, say, a TLC or National Geographic. We produce and own it.'

Gul also has an aviation consulting business that focuses on general aviation.

It's hard to imagine someone with no business background making it big as an entrepreneur. But like a true trailblazer, her achievements don't stop there.

The next year Gul entered politics. She stood as the Aam Aadmi Party (AAP) candidate from Chandigarh for the 2014 Lok Sabha elections.

'I knew it was not a question of *if* but *when* I entered politics,' she explained. 'I was politically inclined ever since college. I didn't want to be on the sidelines complaining about the state of affairs and become an armchair activist. I wanted to be a part of the solution.'

Why at that time?

'It was fait accompli; it had to happen sooner or later for me. If it hadn't happened in 2014, it would have happened in 2019 or 2024. Two things happened that expedited my foray: one, it was no longer necessary to have a famous surname or to come from a political dynasty to enter politics, and secondly, you didn't have to have pots of money to enter politics.'

Why AAP?

'AAP removed the barriers to entry that politics traditionally had in India. I was naturally sympathetic to AAP as a party more than any other party. Also, Chandigarh is my hometown and it already had a candidate for the

Lok Sabha elections who withdrew four weeks before the elections. That's the moment I decided to call up Arvind (Kejriwal), whom I had known from when we were agitating against the Commonwealth Games Scam. He immediately said *theek hai* (yes)! That was it.'

'For me the elections were an inflection point . . .' she added.

It proved to be an inflection point for others as well. Gul did what no one had done before. She campaigned elections on a Royal Enfield, wearing a red leather jacket and jeans, culling a new image for female politicians. It was a bold move that raised as many hackles as applause.

'To begin with biking was an economical decision,' Gul said, when we settled into conversation at her office in Andheri. 'People from all socio-economic strata had opened their wallets to fund my campaign, and we were very conscious about how much we could spend. Biking came naturally to me since I'd learnt it in Chandigarh itself.'

'It was also a powerful symbol of emancipation. When the men in Punjab looked at me, they realized that by giving their wives or mothers or daughters a simple thing like a motorcycle or bike, they enabled them to become more independent. This way we could also have more women on the road and on two-wheelers.' She paused before adding, 'This drives home the notion that equality begins at home with simple things. It's not about bra-burning or shouting from the rooftop. It's about the small things. Women should not have to think twice before stepping out of the house.'

Gul joined politics with the intention to change things. The first part of her political agenda was to fix India's big problem of gender division.

'95 per cent of women are raped by people that they know. This is an important statistic because how do you stop that? A powerful law and order situation could check rapes by criminals, but when your own uncle or brother rapes you, what are you going to do? In India we have no retribution. You can rape with impunity because the girl will not speak up. She will be shamed, especially if she knows the perpetrator, or she will be intimidated by how arduous and tumultuous the process of filing a rape case is.'

With this data in mind, Gul began addressing women's safety for the pertinent and burning issue it is. 'I asked myself, "What can be done to enhance women's safety, especially in cities like Delhi, where AAP has a stronghold?"' she said. 'Through my political campaigns I focused on the safety of women. We focused on finding simple solutions. Better policing was a part of this. We wanted to make the police accountable by circumnavigating hurdles, especially in Delhi.'

A part of this process also involved initiating 'Delhi Dialogues' where Gul met women over 400 personal meetings.

'Women on the ground know what's good for them. For example, they said that once they get off a bus or metro, the part to get home was the big challenge. To combat this they brought forth some unique ideas like last-mile connectivity and better lighting. We decided to introduce something as simple as streetlights. Greater CCTV coverage also worked as a powerful deterrent.

Perpetrators would think twice before touching a woman inappropriately if they knew they were on camera and could be seen. Marshalls on every bus and metro also helped. It's very simple: women want to know that somebody is looking out for them.'

Furthermore, she added: 'Our institutions need to be gender-neutral even if our society is not. A courthouse cannot question what a woman was wearing or whether she was consuming alcohol when she was attacked. Institutions have to herald reform.'

Even in the opaque world of politics, Gul was focused and unafraid to be herself. She was authentic and original. I lauded her efforts as she came out of the stereotypical model of a politician, thus symbolizing women's liberation from normative gender roles. Yet, despite her best intentions and impact, she lost the elections. A school of thought dictated that the men in the community she was campaigning in could have interpreted her biking campaign as rather bold. They would have seen her as someone who could corrupt their domesticated women. Was there a price Gul had to pay for giving a new face to politicians in India, especially female politicians, in a field dogged by male supremacists?

'It's not as if only Bollywood and politics are male-dominated, our society is patriarchal,' she explained. 'Secondly, tokenism and symbolism are both not enough to enable change. We have a problem at hand and we need to solve it at the earliest, or the women of India will never be empowered. How else will we see equal participation in all walks of life?'

Gul's call-out for women to be equal stakeholders with men in society is not an unfamiliar motif. What other ways can women find to be more independent, I asked her.

'Financial independence is the crux for women to become equal stakeholders in society,' Gul replied. 'Our inheritance laws were tweaked to enable women to become equal recipients of their inherited property. But how many women are actually exercising this? I know women who willingly give up their share to their brothers. Why? On top of that, parents don't give their daughters a push to become financially independent. So a woman neither inherits money nor is she enabled to earn it, leaving her subservient as she is without economic freedom. Once we empower women to earn a livelihood, they can choose to become financially independent.'

As she continues gearing herself up for the next political campaign, Gul holds on to her political ideals. 'I'm certainly not politically neutral. I am still a member of the party (AAP) but I have my own set of views, as I am not muffled by a party line, by patriarchy or by a specific agenda. I want to stand up and do something, while reserving the right to say what I want to say. I want to be a real person's role model.'

'Politics is not a career; you don't make money out of it. So, I am a career entrepreneur, a career producer, but I am not a career politician. I need to make a living from other careers, not politics. Therefore, I can be an honest politician.'

Gul has worked hard to understand her role in politics. 'Being in politics taught me to take off a mask. I was able to be who I want to be. Show business conditions you to be aloof, but politics breaks that down and forces you to make eye contact. After all, you can't engage with a voter with dark sunglasses on!'

She also reposes implicit faith in AAP and the party's role in the nation's progress. 'We are a young party and we have made many mistakes. I am sure that we will make some in the future as well. We are more a movement than a political party, and we need to move towards a party of checks and balances. We all know that there is a need to reform how politics is conducted in India. I believe only a disruptive party like AAP has the potential for this reform because the other parties are too deeply entrenched for change. We are learning all the ropes and we are trying to do it while making the system better.'

Will she contest again, I ask her? 'I'll cross that bridge when I come to it, but I am certain that I will be a part of public life over the next thirty years.'

Till then, Gul believes that we need to have more conversations to challenge deeply entrenched patriarchal notions. I couldn't agree more.

In whatever role she dons, Gul has never been afraid to exercise public agency. Despite being an outsider to the world of glamour, Bollywood and politics she dove head-on into them.

'I don't think of myself as an outsider to these industries because I believe they are a cross-section of society.'

I meet Gul again in 2016 when she invites me as a speaker for a women-only festival 'Festivelle' that she is co-curating with actor Shruti Seth. It is then that I learn she's become an aviator. I'm surprised but only a little; this is Gul and she can do anything.

'How did you start flying?' I asked her.

'I always carried a desire to learn how to fly. The seed was planted in Patiala, when I would ride my bike to college and pass by the flying club. A cousin of mine had also done his flying from there, so aviation was something I'd been exposed to. I didn't want a job with an airline as flying was just one of the things I wanted to do in my life. At the beginning, I didn't have money to pursue the hobby, and when I had the money, I didn't have the time, since I was an actor. Therefore, while I began to check all the boxes in my life, flying got left behind. It was only a year after Rishi (Attari) and I got married, that he told me "Why don't you do it?" He pushed my dream from passive to active. I stopped making excuses and got down to it. In 2012, I started learning how to fly in Patiala. In 2015, I switched to Chimes Aviation Academy in Sagar (Madhya Pradesh) because it had a dedicated hobby-flying programme. I got my flying licence in 2016. Even today I try to fly a couple of hours every month, sometimes in Mumbai and sometimes back in Sagar.'

'The way I want to fly is my approach to everything—I feel like it's going to happen and then I make it happen. My first solo flight happened in 2015. It was a momentous experience. I landed after a routine training flight, when the instructor suddenly got off the plane and told me to go alone. I was very nervous and not sure that I could do it. Somehow, I managed a good sortie and even an incredible landing, with the folks at the ATC (Air Traffic Control) clapping and cheering me on.' She smiles as she recalls the memory. 'It was one of the big trigger points in my life after Miss India; it made me feel like I could do anything.'

'The first time I got that kind of real confidence was as an eight-year-old kid when I was able to make a horse canter by myself. Since then I've been setting different goals for myself, and fighting tooth and nail to achieve them. It's like finishing your first marathon, after which you feel like you can finish any marathon. The triumph after the fight instills in you a great sense of self.'

Every meeting with Gul is the beginning of a new discussion. Whether it's feminism, campaigning, flying, motherhood, entrepreneurship, there's never stagnation. She is constantly reinventing herself.

'Why do I have to be one thing? I don't want only one job,' she says to this.

Gul is not afraid to be herself. She has let experience, talent and ability take precedence over aesthetics, age and beauty. She is original and authentic, two qualities that are most difficult for women in India to imbue. Where does her confidence come from?

'It comes from a place of self-empowerment and self-worth. There are many things that I can't do, but I like to believe that I can do everything. I set goals for myself that I think I can achieve, and then I go out and achieve them. I have been never afraid to try anything.'

Who taught her to think this way?

'My family brought me up as an empowered person. My father, in particular, is the architect of my early years. He instilled in me my values, ethics and ambition, while my mother supported his vision for me. He told me to pursue excellence, to never sell myself short, and to never follow a preordained path. In our country, where women are conditioned to have children early, my father would send me articles about women having kids at forty. I remember a letter he wrote to me after Miss India. It said:

Your life is extraordinary and it's going to be so. You need to find small windows to do the ordinary things. Make your peace that you will not be a regular person.'

'My father taught me one simple lesson: if you want to make a mark in society, then every four-five years you have to put in 10,000 hours of additional effort, above your normal work. So, if your workweek is seventy hours, put in that extra work to lead over your contemporaries. Go above and beyond your call of duty. Constantly upgrade your skills, pick a hobby, play a sport, but do something extra. Otherwise, you'll forever remain an ordinary person and never stand out.'

'My father is unbendable, outspoken, principled and super accomplished,' Gul continued. 'He carries the strength to call out what's right and wrong; sometimes even I am unable to take such strong positions. For example, he was the first person to call out the human shield incident in Kashmir, which set off a spark of protest. He is not afraid of anything. During his time as Army Commander Northern Command, he never wore a bulletproof vest. During his entire time in the army, he led from the front and taught by example. It's also something he did actively as a parent. For example, I imbibed my focus towards fitness as a result of him being fit. He would run with me every day till his knees gave way at fifty. He led an exemplary life and inspired me to do the same.'

This is compelling. Women in India are generally not encouraged to exercise public or private agency. They're told that they can't walk on the road wearing this or that. They're told that they must have no identity at home except that of a wife and mother. Unconstrained by the matrix of societal expectations, Gul is rising above these societal norms and barriers, and inspiring others, including me.

'I have come to realize that when as a woman you show the world what you can do, you inspire many other women to go out there and achieve their dreams. There is a voice in my head that tells me that I can do anything, but it's only in recent years that this voice has become loud and I let it be heard. Every woman should feel this way!'

And, they should feel much more. Like love. Gul, in between all these achievements and dreams, married Jet Airways Captain Rishi Attari. 'He was my senior from our boarding school Lovedale (The Lawrence School),' Gul said of him, smiling from ear to ear. 'At that time he was the head boy and I had a major crush on him.' It was only later on that Gul and Rishi met again and fell in love. From what I've seen, and as sappy as it sounds, Rishi seems like the wind beneath Gul's wings. How much of who she is, who she keeps becoming—this fascinating, interesting, accomplished woman—does she attribute to him?

'I am very lucky to have him,' she replied, blushing. 'He has been the second most incredible guiding force in my life; the architect of the second part of my life. We've been together since 2000. He is the person who sees my potential and helps me achieve it..When Savita Bhatti, Jaspal Bhatti's wife, pulled out of the 2014 election, it was Rishi, along with my father, who told me to contest, and even came with me to meet Arvind Kejriwal. He pushed me to fly. Even today, he pushes me to get out of my comfort zone. For example, he pushed me to commit to doing a regular Facebook live video to maximize my social media potential. He is the guy who truly gets me and never lets me sell myself short of potential.'

This is endearing, to hold on to this feeling of love twenty years on.

But marriage and love in India don't come without censure, and in her case these have been constant questions about starting a family.

'I will have a child, sooner rather than later, and it's something I've thought very deeply about,' she said. 'But motherhood is a choice in which a woman should play a big part. She should take the decision about if and when she wants to have a baby. It's her body, after all. Yet, this option is taken away from her for two reasons. One, she is not given a vote. Second, she is under constant pressure from society to deliver a child. What people may not realize is that when you bring a human being into this world, you have to give them time and impart values. The child will not grow up on its own, which was the thought process of the previous generation. I fundamentally believe that the decision to have a child needs to be arrived at by both the husband *and* wife. It's not a one-way street. If either partner is not ready, they shouldn't go ahead.'

Actor Jennifer Aniston had said that women should not be treated like 'walking wombs'. Yet, in India, some of our most seemingly emancipated female celebrities like Lisa Haydon spout tripe indicating that a woman's biggest talent is popping babies. Our society treats someone as less of a woman for not being a mother, despite the fact that our country is in desperate need of population control. Birth control is rarely heard of and babies are born without due deliberation. Advocating sensible family planning, as Gul is doing, is needed to bring about an imperative socio-economic shift.

If we empower women, their choices and decisions will become par for the course, Gul states.

Miss India. Model. Actor. Activist. Fitness enthusiast. Traveller. Politician. Entrepreneur. Aviator. There is no mountain high enough that Gul cannot climb. She's shown us that even the sky is not the limit. And, she's not even forty yet. What's next on her bucket list?

'I've turned a writer and will soon be coming out with a book on fitness. It is a compilation of my fitness lessons and what works for my health, body and mind. The book idea came to me because women would ask me how I maintained myself after marriage. I've been consistently fit over the last decade or so, so being fit wasn't dictated by me being an actor. Fitness enhances my potential because it makes my mind objective, and the endorphins from exercising give me a positive frame of mind.'

Writing deepens and widens my sense of life: it feeds my soul. For Gul, who thrives on expecting the unexpected, I imagine the book will ensconce the same sentiment.

Women like Gul—women who are fearless, women who seize life for all it's worth, women who are not afraid to try anything—will never be forgotten for they'll always make history.

Ankhi Das

Public Policy Director, Facebook India,
South Asia and Central Asia

I liked Ankhi the instant I met her. She is a force, intense and driven, and that is her power. She reflects a live version of that crystal ball with energy tentacles defining its form. Her strong views, and quick admission of what she wants, likes and hates are on the table along with her cup of green tea. There are no two sides to Ankhi Das, who heads public policy for Facebook in the region. If you come to her with five ideas, you return with ten. Ankhi has a voice of her own. She grew up in a home of strong women, where educating the daughters of the family was not a responsibility but a resolve.

While growing up, there were many influencers who shaped Ankhi's worldview. Pre-dominant among them was her maternal grandmother. 'She was a child bride, married at fifteen, like most girls were in her generation. Those were difficult times—the country was grappling with our freedom struggle, much uncertainty and she was married to my grandfather in Dhaka in pre-Partition days. My English-educated grandfather, with sisters who were all college-educated, behaved like a mini-aristocrat family with her. My grandmother was homeschooled after marriage, and though I think my grandfather loved her, she was also subjected to friendly taunts for her inability to read the English *Statesman* newspaper at the breakfast table. She narrated these stories to me to stress how her lack of education crushed her sense of self.' That experience led to her resolve to give a strong education to her daughters, which she did eventually, and Ankhi was the third generation to reap the benefits of that determination.

If feminism is having a voice in your relationship with yourself, then Ankhi is a feminist. Her early ideas about women and independence were nurtured at home. 'Feminism to me means having a voice—a voice in your relationships with others, in society and above all, with yourself. It is a fundamental value of equality and liberty.' There are all kinds forces at work around Ankhi. Her supportive husband, a boy she has raised to be a feminist, and a family that celebrates her achievements and resilience. And then some. As I enter her office earlier at the Taj Mansingh in Lutyens's Delhi (her office has moved to another place since), I am amused by a tiny statue of Lord Shiva placed behind the flower vase at the entrance mantel. I step back immediately, leaving behind comic-like speed lines, kind of surprised by its presence in a social media office. 'That's Lord Shiva; I worship him. He likes women. He supports them. He is a good god,' Ankhi defends his feminist disposition as I ask her about fasting on Monday. 'Parvathi is a strong woman and Shiva celebrates her.' Her office, like her, is no-nonsense. A small conference table enmeshed with wires, a sit-out with books (two of which happened to be mine and I insisted they were there by design) and a couple of simple rimmed poster frames of an Instagram campaign. We order green tea for her and Coca-Cola for me to get down to talking about this book. As on most occasions when we've met, Ankhi is dressed in a neatly draped sari, resplendent with a maroon bindi underscored by a black line. She wears Bengal on her sleeve, as if in a show of support of her defined views, upbringing and strong sense of self-belief. 'In school and in college, I was drawn to social sciences, where I studied about the Bengal Renaissance, the Bengali literary greats and the social transformation of Bengal post-Independence, and in particular, post-Partition (from what is now Bangladesh). Women entered the workforce to deal with the economic hardship caused by the Partition, large-scale economic displacement, and to augment family incomes,' Ankhi reckons. This explains why she is vehement about the idea of economic involvement of women as a way of empowering them. 'Economic necessity in post-Independence India drove a lot of public movements, raising awareness about feminism in Bengal and more participation of women in economic organizations. The deeper I dug into this period, the more my views got defined.'

Today. Facebook has embedded campaigns that transfer knowledge and social tools to women in small businesses. She switches precipitously from a smile to a purposeful frown, animated about her concerns, an eyebrow raised for arched focus, and asserts, 'I ask myself every day: What is my responsibility to support more women unlock economic and social value?'

At her seven-year mark at Facebook, this question has become even more pronounced. Here she deals with women, almost directly because that is the nature of the social network. In millions, in diverse languages, with the hope to use their digital life as an effort towards emancipation, outside the four walls of their homes. The introspection is palpable because there is an opportunity here to use digital tools to change lives and mindsets. 'We have seen farmers and fishermen become more productive by tracking weather conditions and comparing wholesale prices through their mobile phone. Students, who wouldn't otherwise have had access to education, have been able to learn online. For us, it is all about the people. Creating locally relevant content and applications for India's local languages, which every day people in India will find useful. Perhaps it's a service that migrant workers in cities can use to send money to their families in remote villages, or access medical information and counselling in areas where facilities are scarce.'

She is enraged by the slow rate of change that has come to women in Indian society. 'I ask myself, what is this moment that we are in? Justice Leila Seth once told me that when she was in the Patna High Court, there were no toilets for women judges. When she joined the bench, they created a temporary toilet for her. It was in a dingy corner and she had to navigate bandicoots that would spring up at her every time she went that way. She had to cover her head with her sari to protect herself from getting bitten by the bandicoots racing across the dimly lit room. Let's not forget what came before us.' She does not want to forget the sacrifices of women who rebelled to let us have freedom, even for a moment. 'It is due to the struggle of this generation of women that we have the place that we do. We owe it not only to ourselves but others who will come after us.'

But the change she seeks puts the onus on society and its people. 'Creating conditions for success is more important than creating laws. If you look at Raja Ram Mohan Roy, he mounted a huge social movement. It was not just a law that stopped Sati. There was an entire infrastructure he created for social change. This was our history and we can learn from it,' she analyses.

After studying international relations and political science at Jawaharlal Nehru University, Ankhi worked as head of corporate affairs at what was the combined Amarchand Mangaldas (back then a single entity but now separated as Shardul Amarchand Mangaldas and Cyril Amarchand Mangaldas), a law firm in New Delhi. She then took charge of public policy for Microsoft, understanding and handling regulatory affairs in the technology sector. At Facebook, the majority of her efforts are focused on promoting the tech giant's role in India's social and economic growth. These efforts were far less in the spotlight in a non-digital environment and Ankhi draws up the market conditions in which some of them entered the job scene.

'My generation is the college generation of the nineties. I consider this generation to be the first generation to enter the workforce post economic liberalization.'

Choices for all young people, not just women, were extremely limited. Studying humanities back then meant Ankhi, too, had limited choices—mainly academia and the civil services were the mainstay. The economic reforms of 1991 fully played out by the mid- to late-'90s. They opened up new avenues for young people to shape their careers using their education and skills by unlocking huge opportunities with infusion of foreign investments and private capital—unshackling generations from the moribund state socialism of scarcity and lack of opportunity. The share of women in the workforce was less than half that of men during this period but it was rising. Gender equality neither existed on paper, nor as a live debate. Few realized the strength and qualifications women leaders could bring to the boardroom.

'It is our moral duty to invest and demand leadership roles and seats for women at the table in boards, organizations, in our politics and in our families,' she says putting the onus on her own contribution. 'I have always asked myself: why do companies have boards? Because they want to continue to invest in growth and want critical advice. If you value yourself as an asset, you need a personal board. We women, I think, need it more than men do. We demand less and give more. We don't realize that we do that.' There is a long political and economic history to prove that. Exploitation of women during the Industrial Revolution preceded the women's suffrage movement or right to vote in the UK. Modern feminist movements arose from that. While we re-shape our voice and leadership roles, we need support from other leaders. In that spirit, Ankhi absolutely insists on finding mentors, sponsors and connectors who can be agents of change.

She learnt her biggest feminist lessons from men. People who influenced her leadership styles were mentors at organizations where she worked earlier. Shardul Shroff, founder of Shardul Amarchand Mangaldas whom she calls 'one of India's finest post-liberalization minds', has been an abiding and strong influence in her life. He has shaped a lot of her thinking. The other person she admires a lot and has worked with is Ravi Venkatesan, former chairman at Microsoft India. 'People say that women leaders are emotional, they cry in meetings, etc. Well, both these men cry. Every year, at the company meeting at Microsoft when Ravi would talk about doing more for influencing the lives of the poor, building accessible technology for people with special needs, he would cry. When Shardul would talk about bringing on more women lawyers into the firm--something his mother, one of the founders, passionately advocated for—he would cry. That did not make them weak, it made them stronger men and leaders. It demonstrated empathy. A feminist man is a man with empathy and he cries.'

Ankhi's real inspirations came to form when she joined Facebook in 2011. Marne Levine, the global vice-president of public policy at Facebook and now chief operating officer of Instagram, convinced her to join the social media giant, saying, 'she was getting on a giant rocket ship'. And she was. 'It's something I never tire thanking her for.' At Facebook, Ankhi met Sheryl Sandberg who remains an icon for changing the discourse on women at work, and had a singular impact on her. 'Sheryl's biggest contribution has been to establish that it's okay for women to display ambition, to aspire to have the top jobs and work very hard for those. She has given us a new "feminist manifesto". She brings this mission to work every day. We see it in the culture that we have created at Facebook.'

This focus is remarkable in technology with its hard engineering culture where the number of women in leadership roles is still very few. Sheryl's work with *Lean In* and her LeanIn circles is a remarkable way to build global communities of women to help each other have successful and full lives—at work and home. 'I personally am very focused on pipeline development and building the future, while making sure that we are investing in more young women and their leadership in key roles as we grow the company's operations in India. That means having a seat at the table. I always look for an opportunity to involve more women in problem-solving and advocate for them to have a seat at the table.'

In India, the onset of digital has transformed the size of opportunity women have. Today, the Internet is the invisible force, driving the advancement of women. It is helping to give women a voice, involve them more deeply in society and afford them opportunities to be financially independent. 'Take education. Research shows that educated women have healthier families, earn larger incomes, and create more economic growth, yet two-thirds of the world's illiterate are women,' Ankhi explains.[1] The Internet opens up a world of knowledge, from digital books and Wikipedia to online courses. Research shows that when women have access to reading apps, they use them significantly more than men.

'Thanks to the Internet, women can become entrepreneurs. In the last four years (between 2012 and 2015), the number of new women-owned small and medium businesses Pages) on Facebook has increased six fold,' Ankhi shares. 'Kalpana Rajesh, a woman from India, was inspired to start her own business making bridal hair accessories after having done so for years for friends. She started her business in 2012 with three people—herself, her domestic worker and her friend. Today, she employs more than 200 women, working across thirty-six branches from Delhi to Tuticorin, with multiple product lines. She says that without Facebook, she estimates it would have taken her fifteen-twenty years to grow her business to the same size it is today. Not only has Kalpana made a difference to her own life, she has made a telling difference to the lives of more than 200 women who are now earning their livelihood, thanks to Kalpana.'

---

[1] https://bit.ly/2u61rTv.

The Internet also gives women a voice—and makes sure their voices are heard. 'Stop Acid Attacks is a group formed by women who have suffered horrific and scarring attacks, to help raise awareness on the issue and help provide a safe space for sharing stories. This group has more than 700,000 fans on its Facebook Page. We've also seen groups such as Delhi for Women for Safety, Blank Noise (collective against violence against women) and Bell Bajao (a campaign against domestic violence) use social media to champion great causes.'

Empowering women economically isn't just good for them; it's good for everyone. Women employ more women, they act as great role models, they encourage more diversity, they invest in their communities, educate their children and pay back the benefits they receive by helping others. Research shows that countries with more equality in employment and education have lower child mortality and faster economic growth. The United Nations estimates that the Asia–Pacific economy would earn an additional USD 89 billion annually if women achieve their full economic potential.[2] 'Using the talent of our complete population is critical,' Ankhi proclaims.

But India's ground realities are disparate, so much so that gender and feminism are considered subsidiary problems, like an appendix of a book. There is a cultural conflict, a deep, dark and rooted patriarchy that doesn't celebrate empowerment. To get more women into leadership roles, we have to address our

---

[2] https://bit.ly/2N0UV7C

discomfort with female leadership. This dynamic carries over into the workplace, where women walk a tightrope between being liked and being respected—and men do not.' This persistent bias creates a double bind for women that we must bring to the surface, acknowledge and fix. 'Transparency and training are vital. If employees see real, measurable gender inequities in their organization, they will be more likely to work towards solutions. Implementing training so that the employees learn how to identify and counteract gender bias is critical, especially for managers who shape the day-to-day work experience of most employees. Women suffer by having less access to senior-level mentors and sponsors in the workplace than men, and this needs to change. Peer support can be part of the solution.'

Ankhi's journey to discover the feminist in herself wouldn't have been fruitful without the support of her family who encouraged her independent ideas, her views and her career path. 'There are three decisions in my life which I think have been my best decisions—getting married to Soumya, my husband, having Arpan, my son, and coming to work at Facebook. All have been life-defining.'

She is quick to add that the bedrock of a feminist family is the belief that all genders are equal. For her, balancing life, career, family isn't a question only women face. 'It's not a responsibility that women alone should be tasked with. So, whether it is raising a family or attending to a sick parent—caregiving is a gender-neutral role and we need to imbibe that as a society. For only then will we have equality in our homes and more representative workplaces and economic organizations. It's a necessary condition for our progress and healthy societies. I am lucky that I am surrounded by feminist men all around, at home and at work, who fuel me all the time.'

Aarefa Johari

Journalist, Activist

'I don't remember the excuse I'd been given when my mother took me to visit a Bohri neighbourhood at Bhendi Bazaar in Mumbai. But I do remember that we knocked on an unfamiliar door and that, a few minutes later, I was on the floor of a strange woman's house. Someone was holding me down and I was scared. My underwear was taken off and my frock was raised. I had no idea what was going on. I felt confused, anxious and scared. The only preparation I received was my mother saying things like, "Don't worry . . . this will only hurt a little bit . . . this will be over in a few seconds . . ." before the woman brought a blade between my legs. She cut something down there. It hurt and I cried. I don't remember blood, but I have vague memories of being afraid to urinate for the rest of that day. I was only seven years old. I didn't know that the hood of my clitoris had been stolen forever.'

This is what Aarefa Johari remembers of her *khatna*, which is also known as female genital mutilation (FGM) or female genital cutting (FGC). Circumcision is considered a rite of passage among Bohra Muslims and girls typically tend to forget this nicking. Aarefa tried to do the same, but she couldn't.

'While I was aware of it, I didn't ask much more because I was a child. But when I grew up and understood what had happened to me, I was indignant. Even though I was told that only a thin layer of skin had been removed, for me, my clitoris had been snatched away without my consent, at an age when I was powerless to protest or to understand what had happened to me. I knew nothing about sex or my own anatomy or the long-term effect this would have on me. I felt helpless, betrayed and enraged.'

Aarefa, otherwise, takes pride in her community: the Dawoodi Bohras, a small Shi'ite sect from Gujarat, are a wealthy and enterprising business community that encourages women to be well-educated and to work. 'We are proud of being able to balance our modernity and piety, so much so that we consider ourselves superior. Yet, we perpetuate the genital cutting of our daughters,' says Aarefa. 'Worse still, since the community is centrally run by one head, the customs are followed globally; we take them with us everywhere, even when we migrate to foreign countries. Because of this, we keep our lives separate from the rest of the world, even from other sects of Islam. This, to me, is a stark reminder of how close-knit and insular we are as a community.'

Aarefa refused to reconcile to this mode of conformity. She sidestepped the passive resignation of her mother and grandmother, and refused to accept khatna as either an approved norm or the accepted way of life.

'Initially, I was angry only with my mother. I confronted her when I was in college. What was she thinking? My grandmothers were superstitious, true, but how could my mother—an educated, intelligent and urban woman of science—be talked into violating her daughter's sexuality? Didn't she ask anyone *why* this ritual had to be followed through? She always taught me to question everything and value science. So how could she do this to me?'

Aarefa recalls her mother's response, 'My mother had never questioned this practice, especially since male circumcision was also rampant, and she had assumed that it was the same thing for women. She had read a magazine article by an anonymous Bohra woman citing studies that connected male circumcision to reduced risks of getting STDs (sexually-transmitted diseases) and certain kinds of cancer. Because of my indignation, my mother began asking around. Sometime later, she heard from a Bohra friend that female circumcision supposedly serves a similar purpose: preventing uterine cancer in women. For my mother, this "scientific" backing for khatna offered a reasonable explanation for a practice that her religion expected her to follow without questioning. I realized that she had done it out of good faith because when it comes to religion most people have an implicit faith and don't ask questions. This helped me get over my personal resentment. That's when I began to question systemic practices and how things operate within organized religion.'

The justifications used to explain the pervasiveness of khatna outside her home are even more absurd, Aarefa tells me. The most common one is that it is a part of religion, custom and faith, since Muhammad the Prophet has said so. The second most common reason is that since women in Islam are not supposed to be sexual, khatna is done to moderate sexual desires and protect a woman's chastity. Since—unlike the vagina—the clitoris has nothing to do with menstruation, conception or childbirth, and everything with the female orgasm, Bohras identify it as *haraam ni boti*, a sinful lump of flesh, which needs to be removed to keep women 'pure'.

Furthermore, Aarefa has written in www.womeninandbeyond.org what her forty-plus-year-old aunt, a psychology graduate, told her: 'Women have far more sexual urges than men, and it is necessary to control them. Men have to go out and do the hard work; they cannot be having sex with their wives all day. That's why the Prophet has emphasized khatna for girls—if they are not circumcised, they will all grow up to be prostitutes.'

The age-old patriarchal hack, protecting a woman's virtue, is another reason offered by conformists. But Aarefa was not one to allow her genitals to be made the fountainhead of shame. She refused to let them be the placeholder protecting the whole world's honour.

'Everything to do with female sexuality is taboo. Women are not supposed to talk about their private parts. I cannot abide by that.'

There is also the tendency to compare khatna to the prevalence of FGM in some parts of Africa where large chunks of a young girl's genitals are cut up using unhygienic blades, and vaginal openings are so badly sewed up that it leads to fatal infections and death during childbirth.

'This information is also used as a justification,' Aarefa adds. 'My community takes offence when khatna is clubbed under "mutilation" because they think that "our way is different from the African way"; it is better and more hygienic. Since girls are cut less than the boys are on their foreskin, they feel like no harm is being done. The truth is that even if the terminology is different, it is still a form of cutting.'

The ritual, Aarefa says, has no medical sanction. It is typically performed on seven-year-old girls by untrained surgeons who snip away in their living rooms under questionable hygienic conditions, or in small hospitals around the world. 'I had gone to Jamnagar (Gujarat) for a reporting trip where I spoke to an old lady about khatna. She informed me that it was being done in a clinic by a local doctor, only because cases "*bigad rahe the*". It made me wonder how many cases were being botched up? And this is just one town. When you have a midwife with no medical training and a terrified seven-year-old trying to possibly fight the blade, where is the guarantee that only a thin layer will be cut? I have come across Bohra women who've lost their entire clitoris. All these stories remain silenced. Where is the accountability?'

'A non-sterilized environment can become a hygiene issue, but even if the environment is sterilized, khatna is still a non-medical procedure. It is still traumatic. Even if the trauma is forgotten, it can surface later, at the time of marriage and one's first sexual experience. A hospital setting does not take away from the trauma. Performing khatna in a medical setting does not make it a medical procedure.'

Aarefa could not adhere to this fear-based compliance. She felt frustrated and uncertain. What did an incomplete clitoris mean for her?

'Male circumcision doesn't have a negative impact on men's sex lives,' she says when we speak, 'since men will—obviously—not harm their phalluses. Therefore, it is frustrating for me to know that I am deprived of sex in my natural form and my right to a complete body due to social and cultural reasons rooted in patriarchy. Not just me, but every woman who has been circumcised.'

Although there were some stray efforts by women in previous decades—in 1989, Rehana Ghadially wrote a paper titled 'All for Izzat' in *Manushi*, a journal about women and society, and became the first Bohra woman to publicly speak against khatna—the tipping point against this practice was reached in 2011, when someone with the pseudonym Tasleem asked the Bohra community leader to ban this practice through a Change.org petition, that received a lot of media attention.

These efforts made Aarefa realize that normalizing this deeply gendered phenomenon was untenable to her. In 2015, she co-founded Sahiyo, a non-profit collective, with four other women who felt passionately about ending khatna. The purpose was to advocate the values of consent, bodily integrity and a woman's right to her own body and sexuality, using storytelling, community engagement and healthy dialogue. From conducting outreach campaigns to developing a storytelling platform for survivors, Sahiyo aimed to break the silence around the taboo subject and encourage the community to have effective, healthy and non-judgmental conversations about khatna with each other.

'We did the first-ever worldwide online survey of Dawoodi Bohra women on the subject of khatna, and found that there is a prevalence rate of 80 per cent, even though 81 per cent of those surveyed actually want the practice to end. We went on to publish personal stories on our website so women knew that they were not alone. We also started a flagship programme called Thaal pe Charcha, where women from the community come together in a safe space where they can share their experiences and discuss matters that affect them as Bohra women.'

Over the years, more women started reaching out to each other, as gradually other collectives like Sahiyo were formed.

While she showed her community that some cultural practices are nothing but flimsy mantels of subjugation and diminution, Aarefa's outrage was met with more outrage. Her earnest attempts were viewed as monomania that was hijacking and derailing traditional norms. Her actions were painted as destroying and not relocating a way of life.

'While I've not faced direct backlash, a lot of people have. I get a lot of support from a lot of people. Those who disagree with me may tell my mother, but they don't mention it to me directly. Many women are afraid of being socially boycotted by the community if they speak out against khatna. Our young girls face immense pressure from their families to comply to community life. Among Bohras, there is a pervasive fear of being ex-communicated for speaking out against any issue. The truth is that it can get personal. Dissenters can have their entire families ostracized. They may not be allowed inside the mosque or in the graveyard. Their business may be affected, especially if it is tied to the community. Their marriages may not be solemnized and their last rites may not be performed. Therefore, even though there is no diktat for ex-communication in case of khatna, people do not want to take a chance and speak out against it.'

Some khatna defenders have even gone on to form a group called Dawoodi Bohra Women for Religious Freedom. 'Their argument is that khatna does not equal mutilation. They feel that the WHO (World Health Organization) is biased and wrong to include the "harmless nicking" of the clitoral hood under the same term used to describe infibulation,' Aarefa tells me. 'This group aims to dilute Sahiyo's work by discrediting us. They claim that we are not really Bohra because we don't actively dress the Bohra way and don't seem to be as religious. They run vigorous social media campaigns with hashtags like "Sahiyo is not my voice".'

Despite censure, Aarefa did not back down. She understood, as any feminist would, that a woman's right to life and dignity is not contingent on her obeisance to traditions and norms. Her activism became analogous with her identity as a woman.

This marginalization is not unlike some other battles we observe in India; that of the Dalits, the LGBTQ community, and persons with disability who are denied equality. Sahiyo is sensitive to being an inclusive initiative. This begins by translating the content on their website into Gujarati and other vernacular languages so they can reach out to a wider community at the grassroots level.

'We also conducted an investigation into the prevalence of khatna in the Malayali Muslim community from Calicut (Kozhikode). This data was picked up by local Kerala newspapers and led to some positive changes. A political party shut down a clinic where local Muslim girls were cut, while the Kerala health ministry, among other government departments, decried the practice.'

What started as an effort by a handful of women has now become a vibrant movement with hundreds of women speaking out, seeking support, and pledging not to continue this practice on their daughters. They recognize that psychological mutilation does have a place in the hierarchy of legitimate scars. They recognize that the real problem is that the clitoris has been given almost no voice in our cultural—or even personal—conversations about sex.

'The silence on this topic has effectively been broken. Many more women are now speaking out in public about their personal experiences, even in the face of backlash. This has led to a massive upheaval in the community around the world. There is a debate between those for and those against khatna, and the community has had to face this debate and engage with it,' says Aarefa.

There is another angle. The practice of khatna draws parallels with sexual assault on many accounts. In the majority of sexual violence cases, the victim knows the perpetrator. The same goes for khatna: it is often a trusted relative who takes the child for circumcision. Consent in both cases is tenuous but rarely identified. There is secrecy around khatna and the still-pervasive secrecy around sexual assault. Another point about gender violence is that some of these acts have become normalized, as has khatna. The departure comes with the fact that sexual assault is criminalized. So, how does the law treat khatna? As concurrent debate rages on the Uniform Civil Code, where we question whether the legal system can impose the law on distinctive cultural practices, boosted by the Supreme Court judgment on triple talaq, I ask Aarefa whether this can be done for khatna too.

'The legal system can and should have laws that protect human rights from harmful and regressive cultural practices, but what is the nature of this law? There has to be some cultural sensitivity to it,' she says. 'A law like this should be premised on the nuanced understanding that khatna is a social norm (where parents and the community have no malicious intent to harm kids), rather than a law motivated by Islamophobia, right-wing politics, or some sort of patronizing desire to "save" women and children without factoring in their agency.'

'Do we want a law that makes khatna a non-bailable offence, particularly for the parents of these little girls?

Do we want a law that assumes that all parents who do this are bad parents? How do we plan to look after children in such a case, especially in a country that has pathetic infrastructure for vulnerable women and children? Should the government's responsibility be simply to impose a law, or to also get involved in community education and in raising awareness? These are all complicated questions that need to be raised at a wider level, so that the government as well as women from the community can engage with them before a law comes into effect.'

Many countries have, in fact, spearheaded such laws. Bohras have been in the dock for FGC in Australia, where three people of the community were convicted in 2015. This has also happened in the United States, where up to eight Bohras, including doctors and parents, are currently under investigation for FGC. The truth is that FGC is a global issue, present in nearly every country on the globe from Africa to Asia, Australia, Latin America, New Zealand, North America and Western Europe.

'Having a law against FGC is definitely important,' Aarefa continues, 'but the law alone cannot end this practice. It has not been able to anywhere in the world. In many places, it has pushed the practice even further underground. A law can work only when there is a critical mass of people within the community willing to effect change and end the practice, and for that tireless community engagement and raising awareness are crucial. The change has to come from within; people should *want* to end the practice, or else they simply won't, because deeply entrenched social norms are hard to reverse.'

Her point is that whether or not FGC is criminalized, those who undergo khatna do not report it to the authorities for fear of getting their loved ones in trouble. This is the ultimate truth.

What about the current Public Interest Litigation that is being heard in the Supreme Court?

'It is problematic for many reasons,' Aarefa candidly tells me. 'Firstly, a lawyer named Sunita Tiwari, who does not have ties to the community, has filed the petition. Unfortunately, she has not made an effort to reach out to the actual activists of the movement, nor has she found out why we, as activists in the community, have not litigated so far. Her petition is based on cursory online research, and is riddled with factual errors, exaggerations, generalizations and sensationalism. Anyway, now that the case is in court, individual activists from the larger movement have filed interventions; their petitions are more sensitive and accurate. The Dawoodi Bohra Women for Religious Freedom is also fighting back with its own petition, I believe. We'll have to see how the court interprets all of this.'

Aarefa reflects on her long journey with fighting against khatna: 'What started out as confrontation and resentment changed, when I understood the nature of social norms, and how organized religion and patriarchy work in conjunction. I realized that my mother cannot be blamed for it. She is also a survivor. I realized that individuals like my mother—and I—were merely cogs in the wheel of a larger system that uses religion and patriarchy to justify a cultural practice.'

She adds: 'To change a deeply rooted norm that is based on faith is a difficult task but that's what the task is. The blame lies with the system. Khatna is a type of social norm that is violative of a girl's body, but other practices in other communities—like menstrual taboos—are also discriminatory or oppressive. Unfortunately, they are in our cultural ethos and it is difficult to upset the status quo. There will be a time when this will change, as do all social norms. This change will happen as it did with, say, sati or foot binding, which have now become unacceptable.

'We need sex education to go beyond the kind of anatomy lessons, where the clitoris is not described. This is because most girls know the vagina and urethra but have never heard of the clitoris. Bodily integrity, sexual pleasure and consent also need to be included. Bring positivity instead of taboo. The process of change takes time and blame is not going to resolve it. Meanwhile, the work is cut out for all of us and we need to keep at it.'

Patriarchy has been the societal norm in the world we've been born into: a currency we're trying to demonetize. Out of its squandering privileges have been born practices that promote the falsification of gender dynamics. To restore a balance we don't need answers but we need new questions. We need to grow long roots. It will take time to prevail and mature, but which good thing doesn't? Look at Aarefa, for example. Despite being cut, she has pieced herself together to become the fabric of authenticity that our culture sometimes lacks. This is what progress looks like.

Rohini Shirke

Beekeeper, Digital Woman

Rohini Shirke checks her WhatsApp messages first thing in the morning. No, she isn't part of a friends' group getting updated on all the gossip from the neighbourhood. Nor is this about kids, their show and tell, or school notices and parenting. This is business. On most days, she knows how much she will sell and where the delivery is.

Rohini is from Satara in Maharashtra, and was raised to believe that women must only work in the kitchens and become bread earners. At thirty, her life changed when she got a mobile phone. Surfing the Internet put learning, skills and conversations at her finger-tips. This beekeeper went from being a housewife to an entrepreneur, from being reprimanded to earning respect, from being a simple citizen to standing for sarpanch elections. For her, standing up for your own rights and having an ambition is the real definition of feminism. 'Women's empowerment is feminism,' asserts Rohini. The story of this woman is not just of resolve but of resilience, and a great example of how the digital world is transformational for women. While her journey has roots in an empowered home, her growing up was replete with challenges, emotional upheavals, a tough marriage and estranged in-laws.

Rohini was born in Sonawade village, Patan, in the district of Satara in Maharashtra in western India, about 250 kilometres from the metropolis of Mumbai. Her parents lived in a simple mud house. Her family consisted of her parents, an elder sister and a young brother.

Her father was a farmer who experimented with different businesses. He originally had a tiny shop for selling mixed items and stationery, but then he shut that and started farming sugarcane, wheat and peanuts. 'I have a lot of uncles; so after the partition of the property, we had only a few small tracts of land. My mother helped my father and handled the joint family needs and also worked on the farm.'

Her father wanted his daughters to get an education. So, at the age of six, she got admission in a zilla parishadshala (a district-level government school). It was a Marathi-medium school. Satara has nearly 80 per cent literacy, higher than India's average of 74 per cent. But girls don't always make that count. In Sonawade, the extended society of Rohini's home, people were not big on educating daughters. 'Most parents in our neighbourhood didn't quite support education. In our society, people were amused but my father persisted and put us into school.' Rohini's parents both grew up in the neighbouring villages and were familiar with the people. But even that didn't make it any easier for them to put forward their opinions on raising girls. 'In my house, my parents supported us a lot. Village people would think that my parents were spoiling us. They used to try to influence them and reprimanded them for listening way too much to their children's demands.' This made it harder for Rohini and her sister, but it only strengthened her resolve.

From the very start, Rohini was interested in sports and competed in athletics. 'I used to run 100-200 metre competitions. But I had to wear a full tracksuit. Wearing shorts was not even an option. It was of no relevance to people that clothing could slow me down or obstruct my running. People would say to me—"*Kya* you are dressing like a boy?"' She competed up to the zilla level, showing proficiency in her sport. She didn't have a coach and used to run on her own. There were no options to train and no people to encourage her. 'I used to wake up at 5 a.m. and go for running practice about 3 kilometres away. My papa used to accompany me.' When she grew up, her parents got her a bicycle. Once again, the neighbours taunted her parents for being 'too progressive'.

Her parents were criticized for getting her a cycle. For her siblings, things were easier because she herself was a rebel. 'I used to return home and finish homework, and then collect people in the village for badminton and karate. The mohalla women used to scold me for distracting other kids.' This was when she was thirteen-fourteen years old. Around this time, her father was able to convert their simple home to a proper brick house. Unlike many homes in the neighbourhood, Rohini's father ensured they had a bathroom of their own. Many villages have common bathrooms shared among many homes.

While Rohini spent a lot of time playing sports, she says she didn't disappoint her mother with help in the kitchen. This, she says, was a reason why she could have her way while out cycling or racing. 'I have been able to cook a full meal since I was in Class V (about ten years of age). When I used to leave for school in the morning, I would have made the family's meals and washed the clothes before my departure.'

After Class XII, Rohini thought of learning computers to explore job options. She learnt Microsoft's basics in a computer centre in the nearby town. 'It was a lesson in typing. After that, a local centre asked me to teach other children. That was for Rs 500 a month. It was more like voluntary work.'

Despite a liberal upbringing, Rohini says you can only push the boundaries to an extent. She may not have been completely ready when Rohini was married at twenty-one. The weddings in the village mostly happen based on *patrika* (horoscope), and so it wasn't a case of getting to know the boy in any way. When Rohini arrived in her husband's home, the first few months were spent in getting to know the family and making adjustments. But this was short-lived, because as soon as Rohini showed an interest to work and learn the Internet, she was reprimanded. 'After marriage, my in-laws didn't permit me to leave the house because they were of the traditional mindset. I couldn't possibly do nothing. I was getting restless but led a quiet fight.' Rohini even started a community fund, where she could get women together and help them to pool funds. But nothing went well at home.

Like in many Indian homes, having a baby is considered half the solution to family issues. Rohini's was no different. 'I had a baby in 2011-12. Things didn't change even then. I was told to not learn or work outside any more. My in-laws didn't treat me well.' It reached a point where her mother-in-law told her to make a choice—live with them or go to work. 'She told me to leave the house. So I got a house on rent and started learning. That's when I started learning on my own.' Her worked in Pune. He didn't want to involve himself in the family discussions, or he would be seen as taking sides, Rohini explains. 'In our village, people would force him to listen to his family and succumb to social pressure. That's how it was all through. It was only after I started working and proved I could do something of my own that my husband has started supporting me.' The larger family though has not changed, she says. 'I am tired of explaining to my family. Now people's attitudes have changed.'

Her turning point came in 2012. Rohini started a small beekeeping business to produce honey. 'I wasn't doing anything, so I thought I could start something environment-friendly. That's what urged me to think of honey. In April 2012, I went to Mahabaleshwar Khadi Gram to train for ten days.' When she returned, she attempted to set up bee boxes. It wasn't easy. 'I had to learn about the problems that come. The attack on those boxes, and also about the diseases that spread. It was all new to me.' Rohini says she had an ambition to make this work, but it was very hard for her to get it off the ground. Every day brought new failures. Family pressures didn't ease that dismay. She was determined to find an outlet. This came online. 'Then I joined Google *dharmalaya,* where I learnt how to use the Internet. Through digital, I learnt to search how to grow my honey business.'

Her early business lessons were trying. She used to sell honey to neighbours and relatives, which really wasn't the correct test of her business acumen. 'When I started putting the images of my honey produce on Facebook and WhatsApp, friends of my family and those of relatives also started buying honey. Sometimes they would book it in advance. I realized this was working. It wasn't a favour. These were real people buying my product.' She started out selling 25-50 bottles (less than 100 kilograms) of honey; she now produces 500 kilograms of it. 'This time around, in 2017, I ran out of stock.' Rohini is proud that she could build the business on her own. 'I now know how to take care of the boxes, I have learnt about diseases and I have started monitoring the process.'

Beekeeping in India is still taking shape as a full-fledged business. There are few organized farms. As a result, anyone getting into the business does face early challenges. Like this basic one: Rohini didn't have protective suits when she began. It was her hand against hundreds of buzzing bees. With cloth and plastic wrapped, she had to teach herself the tricks to befriend the bees and move them when they are in the right frame of mind. 'It took me many bee stings, patience and courage.'

The lessons eventually paid off. Marketing the honey was her favourite part. She says that made her leverage the Internet to its utmost. 'As I started marketing, I saw I could make small images with little descriptions and send these to people in neighbouring villages on WhatsApp. Now they saw these images, they would come and order honey from me.'

When word spread about her beekeeping, she realized another business opportunity was lurking underneath. Having Googled so many new ideas, she knew that many farmers use bee boxes as a way of sustainability on a farm. 'I couldn't believe I was beginning to think of new ways of doing business. That's what the Internet did to me,' she asserts with a glimmer in her eyes.

'When I started, I knew this was eco-friendly but didn't know that I was contributing to the organic food movement.' The advantage of bees is not just honey. For farmers, bees are the support staff. Having bees helps to increase their agricultural productivity through pollination. Bees are responsible for 80 per cent pollination for the crop, which increases yield by 30 to 45 per cent. Now Rohini builds, grows and sells these bee boxes to farmers.

She says, given that India has smaller land holdings, farmers look for sustainable means to build and grow their crop. With increased conversation on the harmful effects of pesticides, even the small farmer is becoming conscious. 'I have mastered the art of making sustainable boxes which farmers can then use on their tracts of land. It's great to make it into an organic zone; it causes no pollution as farmers put these bee boxes to increase production of the crop planted. I have become the bee box girl in the region.' Rohini's voice has a hop-skip in it. She says nothing beats the thrill of doing something on one's own. Rohini calls this 'everyday feminism', finding something new and turning it into reality.

For Rohini, embracing the Internet was part of a resolve to prove that society must change and let women have equal learning rights. Many times, normative values seem lopsided and families encourage boys to use digital devices but restrict women. In India, very often parents claim giving a phone to a woman would expose her to safety issues and 'bad things'. 'First, no one used to give me their mobile. They would tell me not to take it. They used to say, "You know nothing about using a phone." Then I got trained on how to switch a phone on, how to use the Internet on it, and how to make a call.'

They say, when you empower a woman, you empower a family. In Rohini's case, it was about empowering the village. As she became independent, and saw her business grow, the rest of the women in the village came to her for help. 'Lots of women in my village are tailors, and design blouses. They come to me and ask me to help them with their designs. Some girls who go to college and need to submit projects, they come to me. *Didi mujhe such bataa do Internet mein dekh kar.*' So now she connects regularly with her neighbours to train them when they need her help. 'Via YouTube, I could learn blouse designs like the princess blouse and other designs. So when my tailor friend comes home, we just sit together and look for videos to understand how to make new designs for her customers.' In every village, the two important stops for women, she points out, are the tailor and the local beautician. 'Today that beautician comes to me and together we find new tips for facials, and how we can use local ingredients to make them. Her customers are very impressed, and they too are getting to learn about how to dress better and stay hygienic.' Rohini says her naught childhood of getting people together to do something, is very much alive in her desire to spread the learnings she has. 'If women don't help other women, who will?'

She has become an Internet Saathi with Google and trains people in her village on how to use the Internet to learn. 'These women are from fifteen to fifty. Earlier, college girls would not be allowed to use mobiles. Their fathers and brothers, like mine, would just not give it to them citing safety issues. *Koi bolte the, ladkiya bigad jayengi.* (Some said the phone would have a corrupting influence on the girls.)' Rohini's example has calmed many parents down about such stress points and she is able to explain to them with a greater sense of confidence as to why women must use the Internet.

During Diwali, when the village school asked the kids to make greeting cards, children came up to Rohini to learn. Rohini says she taught the girls projects, *pawan-chakki*, and other assignments on YouTube and that this effort was greatly welcomed by parents in the village since the kids went back more skilled.

While her family issues haven't evaporated, Rohini finds the family has deeper respect for her tenacity and may even come around in the future. One such moment that surprised and shocked her family and the village was when she garnered the confidence to stand for local elections.

'I used to go to train people in Chargaon. One day, on the way, I saw some propaganda and posters, so I thought why not give it a shot.' She fought in the sarpanch elections. A sarpanch is an elected head of a village-level statutory institution of local self-government called the panchayat (village government).

She feels that there are many conveniences that haven't reached her village. This inspired her to stand for elections and see if she could bring some real changes and earn the respect of the villagers. 'I did the campaign through WhatsApp. Images *banaye ache ache aur prachaar kiya*. (We made some good images for the campaign.)' She campaigned for women's rights and made promises about the work she could do for women's empowerment. She didn't win the election. But she came out stronger and more confident about what village politics is about. She says little things can make people win elections in a village. 'I am a woman, so I couldn't put my arm around a man's shoulders and take him to tea or for paranthas. The male candidates could do that.'

Rohini says patriarchy is so deeply embedded in us as a society that we don't yet know how to counter the small, nuanced details of how men lead and win elections. 'As a woman, how could I have gone to dhabas and sat with men as comfortably as another man can? That itself becomes a vote clincher.' What's heartening is that Rohini wants to stand again, and this time, she says, her campaign would include not just her WhatsApp images but also examples of how she has changed lives as an Internet ambassador. 'I want people to know that we can as *saathi*s, change the lives of other women by simply sharing information and being collaborative.'

Rana Ayyub

Journalist

When *To Kill a Mockingbird* by Harper Lee was published fifty years ago, it was banned for making people 'uncomfortable'. Today, the book is considered the linchpin of American literature. History has long taught us that what is the outrage of today can be the benchmark of tomorrow, that the censored of today can be the artist of tomorrow.

This is what I think of whenever I meet Rana.

Regarded as one of India's bravest journalists, Rana possesses a noteworthy and truth-telling voice in the miasma of noise and suffocating intolerance. An award-winning investigative and political journalist, Rana has covered everything from the Liberation Tigers of Tamil Eelam or LTTE in Sri Lanka to terrorism in India, and far-reaching exposés. Her eye is trained to question the blinkered and botched. In her own way, she keeps the flame of watchdog reportage alive. In a country divided by two types of hate, Rana sits bang in the middle, taking bullets for both: women and minorities.

But, as we know, this is not the best of times to be an independent voice. This is a time when writers and thinkers are killed merely for expressing ideas, when fault lines are being drawn between selective silence and selective aggression, when people are prostrating when asked to bend, when there are skewed notions of right and wrong. At a time when international non-profit Reporters Without Borders ranks India among the most restrictive countries in the world for press freedom, how is Rana comfortable being so politically incorrect that even her Twitter handle describes her as such?

'I want to beat censorship and speak out for justice at any cost,' Rana tells me during a candid chat. 'The consequences of this don't matter.'

The truth is that Rana is comfortable with pushing boundaries. A muckraker in the age of regression. An actor in the theatre of the absurd. A harbinger of bravery. We discuss this, her bravery, to which she says, 'I am tired of being called brave. I've realized that those who need to do the tough talking try to shoot from my shoulder by making me out to be the brave one. They want to abdicate themselves of all responsibilities, so they find a convenient "brave" hero. I fight back because I cannot sleep with lies on my conscience. That is a selfish attempt at unburdening myself. That is not brave.'

But it takes more than one woman's courage to shake our system. We're still dealing with problematic narratives and agendas, where freedom of speech has met a fate similar to that of the Govind Pansare's and Narendra Dabholkar's (both rationalists were shot dead for airing their views). Is she scared for her life?

'I will die when I have to die . . . there is a time for all of us. Till such time I will keep telling the uncomfortable truth, as much as I am detested for it. Remember, history is kind to those who have fought and challenged prejudices. There are periods in Indian democracy where we see the stifling of voices, but it doesn't last long. Some of us are fighting a rather unpopular battle, but I think it is the right thing to do. We have somehow managed to write and say what we want to in the limited space.'

Today, in the time of dichotomy, the Taj is portrayed as a symbol of Mughal brutality, Tipu Sultan is no longer the hero who died fighting the British, and our states are becoming like the new Republic of North Korea. These smokes and mirrors exist in the digital space as well. On one level, social media is empowering women today. It has enabled me to connect with so many interesting women, and reach out to, say, Rana, whom I may have otherwise never met. But it's also coming under the heavy hand of fundamentalism, censorship, draconian restriction and polarization. A woman online with an opinion is an easy target, especially in today's environment.

Rana's social media presence has questioned this regressive state of affairs. For that, as is the *agni pariksha* for most women with opinions online, she faces the daily threats of rape, acid attack or incarceration. I ask Rana, who is probably one of India's most trolled women on Twitter, how she deals with trolls. 'Initially it used to bother me quite a bit. Then I got used to the idea of being trolled every day. There was no logic to any of the criticism levelled against me. Many of these trolls are paid to intimidate, and they are doing their job. I tried to reason with them but there was no point. They had a problem with women . . . they had a problem with someone who had a particular political ideology, somebody who was anti-bigotry, somebody who was outspoken where religion and Islamophobia were concerned. It didn't bother me, but sometimes they would text me during a TV debate saying, "We know where you are . . . at the NDTV studio. When you step down, we have our people." I used to get phone calls from random private numbers. At that time, Prithviraj Chavan was the chief minister (CM) of Maharashtra, so I filed a complaint in the CM's office. I got his officers to investigate, and they asked me if I wanted a revolver for which they'd get a licence (she laughs). But I said, "No, that's it. I just want you to know that there is a problem here. If something happens in the future, there is a case, as there were people who were threatening me."' Rana pauses. 'But now it doesn't bother me as much. I don't read the reactions. I tweet my point of view. They do not threaten me. In fact, sometimes they even amuse me. It's an interesting time to be on Twitter.'

Of course, sometimes this line is crossed, and Rana is forced to react. In April 2017, she posted screenshots of private messages she'd received from UAE-based Indian, Bincylal Balachandran. The messages were abusive with sexual overtones. The UAE government immediately revoked the man's visa and had him deported to India.

'A lesson for those who harass us; we will drag you out of your ratholes,' Rana tweeted in appreciation of the UAE's reaction. And, 'Hope we in India set a similar precedence of zero-tolerance towards harassment.'

So what does it mean for a woman in India to be fearless and courageous, and not conform to stereotypes?

'It's been very difficult. I've been called a jihadi and a Naxalite, among other things. After I broke the Amit Shah story, which sent him behind bars in 2010, I was in a hotel room and they tried to implicate me in a bribery case. At that time, I began to get random messages on my phone. I changed fifty SIM cards in a matter of two months. I went into hiding for a year. It was really difficult. After Amit Shah became the party president, I did a column for *DNA* but the story was pulled down under pressure. We say it is the worst time to be a journalist, but I say it is the best time since we need dissenting voices. This is the time when your journalism is being tested. This is the time when you will come out with flying colours if you stick to your journalism and the truth.'

This exposé was featured among one of "The 20 Greatest Magazine Stories" across the world (*Outlook India*), and won the coveted Sanskriti Award for Excellence in Journalism in 2010. Rana adds that she will continue to clamour not just for objective investigation of the 2002 Gujarat riots, but also for the 1984 Sikh genocide and the 1992 Mumbai riots.

Is there a price she has had to pay for her opinions?

'In a sense . . . yes. There is constant advice from friends and family—"don't go that way" or "why don't you be a little low-profile?" or "why don't you stop tweeting your political opinions?" I've been labelled anti-Modi or anti-BJP for the work I did on the Gujarat riots and the fake encounters. I was in Gujarat as a human rights worker when the riots took place. In a way, it made me who I am as a journalist: somebody who is constantly seeking justice. I'm not the only one doing this, but it drives me to do my reportage. This is the price we pay for being outspoken in times like these, in the times we live in.'

However, Rana is not partisan in her reportage. 'The fact is that my criticism against the Congress about the 1984 riots was equally scathing. No one remembers that.' Rana also clarifies that she admires BJP politicians such as Smriti Irani whom she calls 'very articulate' and Sushma Swaraj who, according to her, is 'very well-read'. One cannot claim that there is no love lost there. 'All I'm doing is speaking out against what should be spoken out about and what the government is doing wrong. If it were the Congress regime, nobody would have bothered to point out my criticism of the government.'

While I am not here to discuss her political views, the truth is that Rana as a feminist conflates Rana as many other things: journalist, author, activist, speaker and spokesperson. There can't be one without the other. In fact, if I had to write Rana as a character in my novel, I would find her indescribable.

So, I begin simply: does she consider herself a feminist?

'I come from a family where my brother and father are bigger feminists than I am,' she replies simply.

What does feminism mean to her?

'I believe in standing up for women whose voice needs to be heard, and to make women more aware of their rights,' Rana says. 'I believe in going to Mohammed

Ali Road (in Mumbai) and telling families to educate their daughters. That is important. Or taking workshops in Kashmir, and spending time asking girls what they want to do, educating them, and helping them out with admissions. I've done that for a couple of girls. Feminism is not about writing articles or making rhetorical statements on Twitter. Unfortunately, that's the case now. Feminism has come to be about this stereotypical notion that we have.'

We both also agree that feminism is not this skewed version of bashing men. It's very important for a gender-equality movement to involve men as equal stakeholders in the process. Men need to be a part of this dialogue.

'Feminism cannot and should not be about male bashing,' Rana corroborates. 'There are many men who are bigger feminists than we are. My problem is,' she adds, 'why do men have to be wrong for me to be a feminist? If someone writes something praising the opposite gender, it creates such a furor. This is wrong.'

We both take a well-deserved moment to discuss Canadian Prime Minister Justin Trudeau who called for boys to be raised as feminists in order to change the 'culture of sexism'.

'Feminism is simply about giving women the same space that men occupy and respecting them for who they are. It is about the respect and status that a woman deserves. This is achievable with the active support of men, and not necessarily by antagonizing them. We need to respect men and take them along in our fight for equal rights.'

Rana feels feminism is not just one thing. It can be different for different people, depending on their situation. 'It is because we have attached generalized stereotypes to feminism that people don't like the word.'

But, like me, she doesn't give in to the sense of apology that has come with feminism becoming a dirty word.

'My problem is with the antonym for feminism that I am told roughly translates into women who are not supposed to raise their voices or have an opinion, but to polish the shoes of their husbands. I am unable to understand this skewed definition of feminism.'

The current trend of people, even women, refraining from identifying themselves as feminists and instead calling themselves humanists is an outcome of equating feminism with male-bashing. I strongly believe that people who pander to popular sentiments and define themselves as humanists instead of feminists, should take a strong hard look at themselves and ask whether feminists don't harbour humane feelings. By being politically correct, we are further pandering to the very sentiments that subjugated us to begin with.

Rana agrees with me, 'I do not like this concept of a "woman of steel". I mean . . . it sort of implies that you can hurt women as much as you want and get away with it. Why should that be the case? Why should women not display their emotions in public? Why should they not be vulnerable? These stereotypes only defeat the purpose of feminism.'

This disdain for feminism has also been fuelled by the increasingly popular belief that women have often cried wolf—in false dowry or rape or domestic violence cases—just to prove a point or get some man in trouble. We can't deny that a handful of women are misusing laws and trapping men in a judicial maze; but more than men, they are making it difficult for the majority of women with genuine cases. Are these handfuls of women taking it to the extreme?

'I know this is not a popular opinion, but just like some laws for women are misused by them, men also misuse laws. Having said that one cannot make a blanket statement that women in our country are free to do what they want.'

This brings me to a point we rarely ponder: that we should be discussing 'responsibilities' associated with feminism. Some of these responsibilities come with owning our decisions, whether personal or professional. I maintain that a woman should choose the man she marries carefully. She should look at his family, especially her mother-in-law and sister-in-law to be, to see the way they are treated and the way they treat her. A woman needs to ensure that she enters a family that will respect her and enable her to reach her potential. Responsibility begins with looking at women as human beings, and not as a 'devi' or a 'devil'. It also extends to dissociating Indian feminism with the more deeply embedded notions of feminism in the Western world.

Rana is equally wary of this, 'It is unfair to compare Indian feminism with that of any other race and ethnicity. On top of everything else, women in India have had to fight caste- and religion-based barriers. Despite this, some of the most phenomenal Indian women have participated in the Bhakti movement, they have become doctors, and they've fought during wars. We had Savitribai Phule, who fought for issues of caste, education and social upliftment. We had Abadi Bano Begum, who participated in the Indian freedom struggle, like Annie Besant. Yes, the West has given us some very progressive women writers like Virginia Woolf and Adrienne Rich, and one should be proud of what they wrote, what they stood for, but the problems of their milieu and their conditioning were very different from ours. One has to understand that over the last two hundred years, feminist discourse in India has been shaped by our colonial past.'

In the professional sphere, it is known how difficult it is to be a female journalist in India. As a female reporter, what did she face in the field that she wouldn't have had she been a man?

'When I entered journalism, I was working for a news channel that I would not like to name. They asked me to concentrate on stories of lifestyle and entertainment. If there was the occasional rape case, I would be sent along with a male reporter in case the victim did not want to speak to a man. But I was hugely interested in politics and persevered. I came through.' She pauses. 'But see, I am from an urban city and I have a background . . . the situation for women journalists in rural India is far worse. They face discrimination and harassment. They are made to do stories that can be easily done by interns; even the senior-most reporters face this. A journalist from Bhopal told me that the only time her boss calls her is when there is a rape or molestation case. On top of that, they get harassed outside the office. We hear about journalists being killed in Uttar Pradesh and Madhya Pradesh. They have a tough space to work in where they are constantly under threat. Journalists from the rural areas are truly the real heroes. These are the women who deserve our respect. Most of us women in the media have fought a tough and unpopular battle to achieve our space under the sun. That for me is feminism. To fight for what is rightfully yours.'

In her decade-long career in journalism, during which she's worked with top news channels in the country and as an editor at *Tehelka* magazine, Rana considers the low-key Meera Jatav, the editor-in-chief of *Khabar Lahariya*, as one of India's foremost journalists. 'I also consider her my favourite journalist. I met her at a women's conference in Bihar. She is not very educated but she runs this enterprising project alongside twenty or thirty other women to bring out the best stories. She is a phenomenal woman.'

Phenomenal she is, for I find out that only women reporters run *Khabar Lahariya* across several districts of Uttar Pradesh. Through a print edition in Bundelkhand and varied digital platforms, the news portal claims to reach 3,00,000 people a month in some of the most remote regions of north India. Considering the harassment female journalists face in India, this is nothing short of an incredible achievement.

I realize another thing: While Rana's opinions make headlines, the woman behind the opinions is little known.

The childhood of a girl makes her the woman she is today. I can't imagine Rana as anything less than a fiery and opinionated child. I wasn't, she laughs. 'In fact, I was an introvert. I hated going to school. I would call my Mom and cry. I would not talk to the boys at school. I was a shy kid; so much so, that when I was in the seventh grade, my schoolteacher called my mother to say, "This child will not complete her Class X." I got comfortable only when I went to a girls' college (SNDT Women's University). It was only when I enrolled for journalism and filmmaking in my postgraduate days that I changed. I was making my first film on madrasas. At this time we were an all-women's crew who would shoot in madrasas across the country wearing shorts and jeans. This was when my confidence came to the fore and I became more political. I interviewed people from the VHP (Vishva Hindu Parishad) and RSS (Rashtriya Swayamsevak Sangh). It was an interesting time.'

What has formed and shaped Rana's opinions to the force that they have now become?

'I was tired of being a chicken, of being a recluse. On an impulse, I went to Gujarat during the 2002 riots as a relief worker and that changed everything. Everything. If 1992 made me aware of my identity as a Muslim, 2002 gave me a purpose. For the last few months, all that I have been doing is reading about black American history and the 1984 carnage. My helplessness in the face of prejudice forces me to be who I am today.'

Her rise hasn't been powered by dynasty or nepotism. It has been created by herself and for herself.

'I come from a borderline communist family,' says Rana. 'I was raised in a household where my mother was as qualified and as successful as my father. As a result, I was treated the same way as my brother—given the same things and the same opportunities. Equality was handed to me on a platter, so I feel very strongly that equality begins at home.'

In 2017, Richtopia ranked Rana number 83 on the 'The 250 Most Influential Women Leaders in the World'. Using various metrics from Twitter, Facebook, Wikipedia, YouTube, LinkedIn and Instagram, the list featured the likes of Hillary Clinton and Oprah Winfrey. Rana has certainly come a long way from the shy kid that she was.

But international recognition may be a sideshow in the context of her achievements. Whenever I've interviewed Rana, I have been clear that we don't want a hagiography. It would be a disservice to her. So we touch upon a subject that is the elephant in most rooms. The Islamic world, which is in the throes of battling two wars: one within their ranks in the form of Daesh and some other terrorist outfits, and the other of growing Islamophobia around the globe. How does Rana, a proud Muslim, tackle this divisiveness?

'It was the 1992 Mumbai riots that made me realize for the first time that I was a Muslim. I was nine years old and my sister was fifteen. I had posters like "Chalo Ayodhya, 6 December" stuck on my door. We had acid bottles thrown into our flat. It was scary for me. As Mumbai burned, our Sikh neighbours, a family almost unknown to us, kept my sister and me hidden from rioters for three months. I guess this experience made us political at an age where ideally we should not have been political. Due to this, I became more aware than most of my colleagues. I started watching NDTV news reports and election debates from the time I was ten or eleven. I guess I've become more political because of the circumstances that I was surrounded by.'

How has her identity as a Muslim woman changed through her work?

'Islam was at the core of my upbringing, though I was not a very religious kid. Even today, I don't offer *namaz* five times a day, but I will fast for the thirty days during Ramzan. For me, religion is about compassion. It has made me the person that I am. I've taken the good things out of it. Growing up, I learnt about Islam and its conflicts, like 9/11. As a practising Muslim who was well read, educated and who has a voice, I needed to speak out against Islamophobia. The first column I wrote was about my memories as a child during the Mumbai riots. During the Charlie Hebdo attacks, I pointed out that the French have my condolences but not my apology. I feel like my community is being targeted for reasons that are not right. Therefore, while religion is not the source of all my writing, it does inspire me. When I see injustice around me . . . not just against Muslims . . . but even say against Dalits . . . I speak up. Somehow those stories get swept under the carpet or don't get enough traction because of my surname. But I continue to wear my surname on my sleeve. For me, the atrocities committed against Dalits and Muslims is something I am keen on fighting and writing about.'

This is the kind of work that led Rana to be named among the "50 Most Influential Muslims in Post Independent India" by the Mid-day group.

When the fragility of many communities is spawning the politics of intolerance, how is her religion shaping her worldview and who she is?

'I come from a very progressive family. My father was a part of the Progressive Writers' Movement (The Anjuman Tarraqi Pasand Mussanafin-e-Hind) and a leftist. Despite this, he was very religious. He was surrounded by the likes of Kaifi Azmi and Faiz (Ahmad Faiz); they would be drinking and he would be offering his namaz.'

I note then that I've never seen Rana wear a hijab (veil). Is this her statement of rebellion?

'I don't believe in wearing a hijab,' she says. 'Neither does my mother or any woman in my family. That said, I do not detest other women wearing it. Whether it is a Sikh woman, or a Christian nun, or a Muslim woman, what they wear is a matter of choice.'

'On many occasions when I am travelling in Muslim-dominated areas, my friends or colleagues expect me to cover my head. I don't do it because I do not want to do it for people. Why should I, as an adult, have my choices dictated to me? My non-conformity to cultural practices could be seen as offensive, but I am what I am.'

There is no hyperbole in her response, or work.

'I want to point out that my rage doesn't extend only to my community. There are many like me, especially in rural India, who are doing phenomenal work. I was in Gadchiroli (in Maharashtra) where these eighteen or nineteen year olds were being arrested under UAPA (Unlawful Activities Prevention Act) for sedition for reading (B.R.) Ambedkar. They came out of jail and went on an awareness campaign. These are phenomenal women, but their work doesn't come to the fore. What I'm doing is putting their voice on the forefront. I'm just a messenger since the phenomenal work is actually being done on the ground by these activists.'

The most dangerous phrase in our language is 'but we've always done it this way' and it's great to see one woman fight the status quo.

'Keep fighting this, Rana,' I tell her, 'and keep inspiring.'

I will, Rana promises, and we move on to another thorny subject: her turning into an author. In 2016, Rana wrote a controversial book *Gujarat Files: Anatomy of a Cover Up*. It delves into the underbelly of institutions and top officials involved with the 2002 Gujarat riots, fake encounters and the murder of the state home minister Haren Pandya. The book was a result of her solo investigations. Through an eighteen-month undercover operation, Rana posed as Maithili Tyagi, a filmmaker from the American Film Institute Conservatory. The work was conducted with minimal resources amid threats and intimidation, she tells me. She adds that the book contains transcripts that Tehelka, a magazine where she earlier worked, withheld from publication. Publishing the book proved to be difficult, Rana narrates, as not just one but two major publishing houses backed out at the last minute.

'Some of the most well-known editors refused to publish my book, giving frivolous excuses. So I took a gold loan and a personal loan, and self-published the book. The facts of the book speak for itself. In two weeks *Gujarat Files* was an Amazon bestseller. Almost twenty months into publication, the book is out in twelve languages and has sold a lakh copies. Truth indeed has takers,' Rana tells me.

She is defiant in the face of criticism for the book. If accused of giving a warped account of the Gujarat riots, Rana says, 'By dragging me to court, or putting me behind bars, the accusers know they would be liable to be questioned in court. That may be why I'm still roaming free.'

The book won her the Shining Light Award (2017) by the Global Investigative Journalism Network in Johannesburg.

'This award is my answer to naysayers. The fact is that I won it in the presence of 1300 of the best investigative journalists and luminaries from across the globe,' Rana says. 'It felt good especially because the lit fests in my own country refused to acknowledge the book, while news organizations did not wish to talk about it.'

In a world where karma is a Black president, a female Prime Minister, a mixed-race divorced Princess, Rana's recognition feels the same.

At a time when our collective consciousness has been shocked by the horrific treatment of women across the country, women like Rana are a compelling reminder that women are neither to be pitied or censured, changed or controlled; they are to be celebrated in all their emotional, empathetic, intuitive glory. For it is the brave, the bold and the beautiful who start conversations that really matter, and I'm glad that the brave, bold and beautiful Rana is doing just that.

Sorabh Pant

Comedian

He calls himself yet another Indian feminist male. Raised by an independent, ambitious and driven mom, he nearly always has to explain to people what he means by that. 'A man who simply wants equality for men and women. I mean how difficult is that?

'I don't think I need to experience something to be empathetic, just as I don't have to be in a war zone to understand what people there are going through.' Sorabh Pant says we are trying too hard to crack the gender code. There is a problem because India is a supremely unequal society. 'One just needs to have an open mind and talk to many people.' He is surprised it takes a lot for people to even absorb the reality. Sorabh says there are many men who champion and support the need for an equal world, it's just that we need to find them and make them work for this cause. 'What I have realized is that the number of men who treat women well are definitely not in the minority.'

Sorabh Pant is one of the founders of East India Comedy with hundreds of shows to his credit. He feels that feminism has an important place in Indian society right now, and in his own way, he has found the answer through comedy performances. Viral videos, raising serious questions through a funny act, or simply showcasing the extremes of human behaviour towards women—all have given agency to a dialogue that was otherwise relegated to gender conferences, or even NGO meetups. Comedy has been given a new outlet for taking conversations to the masses. And at a time when they are all ears.

The starting point is unequal. The definitions of feminism are different for different people, Sorabh says as he explains his version. 'It's about *opportunity*. I think that is the key in this conversation. Your gender should not come in the way of you having the same opportunities as anyone. Post that: it's all good.'

He grew up being a comic, not a doctor or engineer, as many of his generation did. His parents, both of whom were working, left the children to make their choice. And stick with it. 'I think the problem was I was allowed to do what I wanted. I have always made simple decisions in my life, and they are often based on "if this is going to be fun", and then I will figure out how to make money out of it. I was able to make people laugh. And that was my inspiration.'

The problem in India is deep-rooted, and stems from a patriarchal society most of us have grown up in. Right from school, boys are encouraged to play sport while girls are asked to pick up knitting in SUPW. Sorabh says one merely has to enter an engineering college and see the gender ratio—that's where it starts. 'I was writing standup inspired by going to engineering colleges and discovering the skewed gender ratio. And discovering it's about opportunity. Nothing else.' He says all it takes is to superimpose this scenario in all walks of life. From CEO cabins to panel discussions to so many offices, all have skewed ratios. Opportunity is the key.

'It's a pretty simple thing: treat people fairly on the basis of who they are, not by what type of genitals they have.'

There is a great deal of interest in how messaging could empower the movement. Just as there's interest in how comedy could potentially be a great tool to remove taboos in Indian society around the work feminists do.

Sorabh, born in the 1980s, is by definition a millennial. He finds this generation most experimental, and credits the surge of comedy to people's desire to be gutsy and bold. He started work as a TV writer. By his early thirties, Sorabh knew standup was his forte. In 2008, he met up with Vir Das, who was an early starter in the Indian comedy scene. His debut comedy show, called *Walking on Broken Das*, was the opening act for Vir Das's show. Later, he set up his own firm, a touring company called East India Comedy. *Pant on Fire* was his debut solo, and it was a super hit—that got him thinking of expanding his own team.

EIC collaborated with actors Neil Bhoopalam and Meiyang Chang for a video in 2014 titled 'I'm Not a Woman'. In this video, Pant and the others apologize to Indian women because the country is unsafe for them. Pant's work puts the spotlight on the chinks in how Indians perceive cultures, religion, sex, women, arranged marriage, rape and more.

Sorabh wrote a book on the critical issue of women and safety. '*Under Delhi* is about a woman in Delhi going after rapists. It's very angry and dark, yet funny.' His writings have previously dealt with rape. 'It was from a woman's POV, and involved a lot of research and talking to women about their experiences with attacks. It was really depressing. Not a single lady I spoke to said she hadn't been physically assaulted: in bad or terrible ways. A lot of what I said in the book, I later realized, was emotional rather than logical. But, I stand by it.' In this book, he reflects on what it means to be a man and an advocate of women's rights in today's age. 'Finding jokes and light moments in that novel was a challenge, but I did find a way, and people thought it was funny and angry—which was perfect.'

In the last few years, Sorabh's comedy has picked up burning issues like the high tax on sanitary pads in India, the country's obsession with fairness creams, racism and more under his *Rant of the Pant*. 'I also did one about marital rape, which got the predictable response from trolls, but I still believe it offered a relatively balanced approach to the issue from an Indian perspective.' Sorabh has performed for the opening of Wayne Brady's tour to India in 2011 and followed that with his act for American comedian Rob Schneider on his worldwide tour.

Having done so many shows, how convinced was he about making change happen? Was comedy moving the needle on issues in society? 'It's very rare for comedy to "fix" or "remove" taboos. It can make people aware of them,' Sorabh says. In a world where storytelling is becoming key, the conversations matter. With digital, they can be widespread too. 'With *Rant of the Pant*, I covered a bunch of those topics. I'm not sure the world changed. But possibly a few million people thought about a topic from a different PoV. Or maybe were reminded of topics they had heard about.'

Growing up he constantly found himself questioning what made him a feminist. In his family, women always had a point of view and a voice in every discussion. 'In general I have been surrounded by women. They were all very strong women. Especially my mom and my grandmother. It has put the button of empathy inside me. I think if men spend more time with strong women, that could be one way to mould the feelings of people around women. Women rise up from tough situations far better than men do.'

And now, being married, he says he has to be with someone who has a perspective of their own on things. 'I'm attracted to women who are not just funny, but snarky and sarcastic. I love how they make men squirm. What attracted me to my wife was the fact that she got my jokes (and she's hot).'

He wonders why feminism is made into such a big deal. 'Not sure why it has a weird name these days. It's just about having respect for women. We must stop all crimes against women.'

Sorabh says being 'yet another feminist male' comes with a weight he often needs to battle. Men often tell him that all his feminist work is to try and cash in on a trend in the country.

The recent and massive campaign around the world, #MeToo, focused on uncovering cases of sexual harassment after one woman exposed Hollywood's top producer Harvey Weinstein. 'The campaign made me feel extremely depressed about the state of affairs. You speak to every woman in India. And I mean every woman in India. They've had some instance of either molestation, sexual or physical abuse, and in far too many cases, rape. For people who think this campaign is hogwash: talk to women around you and let me know.'

Sorabh credits social media for taking these issues to the mainstream. 'A lot of feminist movements have been triggered by social media: which is great. It has helped bring awareness to the depth of issues. So many of these movements were not considered a big deal for whatever absurd societal reason, and shining a light on them is unbelievably important.'

He does warn that social media campaigns come with caveats and a desperate need to fact-check. 'I do believe the Kangaroo Court of social media for any "crime" should not imply criminality. And I mean this for any crime. Not just for crimes against women. We need to be wary and do thorough research before passing our judgements. And continue fighting this fight that affects not just 50 per cent (as some say), but 100 per cent of the population.'

Shree Gauri Sawant

Transgender Activist

Shree Gauri Sawant enters my home on a wet December evening in 2017, when unseasonal rains are lashing Mumbai. I am breastfeeding my newborn daughter and sit in front of her with a nursing cover. She closes her umbrella and remarks, 'There's nothing in there that I haven't seen before. Even I have breasts.'

This is Gauri—brash, outspoken and unapologetic. I like that. I dispel the cover. Motherhood has made me more comfortable with my body—at its most misshapen—than anything else in the world. So has Gauri. She coos at my daughter and we discuss what being a mother means.

'Having a uterus doesn't make you a mother,' she says. 'A mother does not have a gender. A mother can be a man, woman, gay or lesbian. A mother is a mother. You don't have to label her.'

Such powerful words stated so simply. Gauri understands motherhood well.

I state this as something remarkable because Gauri was born into this world unwanted by her own mother. 'My mother got pregnant at the age of thirty-two, after a gap of ten years from her first child. She wanted to abort me in the seventh month and took an abortion pill. But I didn't die, and the doctor told her that I was so strong that I couldn't be destroyed even if slammed against a wall.' She points to herself; 'Maybe that's why I am breaking walls in real life. And maybe it was my mother's indecision about me in the womb that shaped my gender confusion outside the womb.' She laughs.

Gauri was born, in her own words, into the wrong body: as a man. Her name used to be Ganesh Sawant. And it is this roll of the dice that proved to be most troublesome for her.

'I didn't feel like a hijra or a girl,' she says, 'but I knew I had some unusual traits. I plucked flowers and made lipstick out of it. I carried my mother's hanky everywhere. I never played with boys of my age. If I even tried to play cricket, I would be teased. So I only made friends with girls and played *ghar-ghar* (house) with them. People around me began to notice that I was better suited to be a woman. During a *koli* dance at school, even the teacher told me to play the role of a girl.'

She recalls that as a pre-pubescent boy, she would pluck leaves from the *ajwain* (carom seeds) trees and cut them into little rotis (bread) with the caps of Thumbs Up bottles, or collect *sing-dana* (raw peanuts) and pretend boil them in a cooker.

Gauri felt so much like a woman, she claims, that she would sit down while peeing. 'We had gone to Ratnagiri where we stopped by the fields to take a leak. When I squatted, my Mama (maternal uncle) kicked me from behind and said, "Stand up and pee like a man." I was a woman to that extent. It came naturally to me.'

Her mannerisms did not bode well with her family life.

Born into a conservative Maharashtrian family in Pune, Gauri tells me that her father was a police officer. For him to align his son's gender identity confusion to his macho environment was too big a leap. 'We lived in *sarkari* quarters surrounded by cops. My father was very embarrassed of me. He used to get angry and hit me. After he found a love letter I had written to a boy in school, he stopped meeting my eyes. He told me not to behave like a girl. When I started growing my hair long, he stopped talking to me. He was convinced that one day I would bring shame to the family name.'

Gauri says that she got no love from her family while growing up. Life outside the house was not easy either.

'Once we went to someone's house in a nearby village,' Gauri recounts. 'Two people inside kept staring weirdly at me. Without saying anything, they were teasing and bullying me. It was the first time in my life that I felt dirty.'

I understand. In our world, boys and girls are put into gender boxes. I tell her about the gender ascriptions that are already being prescribed to my newborn daughter. A nanny who worked at my house was upset that a lot of my baby's clothes were blue. I should only let my daughter wear pink, she tittered. I refused the suggestion. An elderly neighbour said that my three-month-old daughter would look like a boy unless I made her wear earrings. I refused to pierce her ears. A child's identity should not be defined by stereotypes. Gauri felt the same way.

As puberty struck, Gauri began feeling attracted to boys. Due to a lack of awareness, she didn't know what being gay or possessing a certain sexual orientation meant. She was simply following her heart's calling.

'At fourteen, I was very hairy, like Anil Kapoor, but even then I knew that I wanted to be a girl! When I was growing up, people wanted to dress up like Madhuri Dixit or Sridevi, but I would watch (singer) Usha Uthup on Doordarshan and say I want to be like her. I loved the way she dressed in saris and bindis.' Around that time, Gauri started cross-dressing. But seeing his son in a sari and bindi was too much for her father to bear. To appease him, Gauri took a middle route and began to wear kurtas that she felt were gender-neutral.

'Some people misunderstood my outward appearance. I remember that during a college *lavani*, I was told to play (popular Marathi actor) Ganpat Patil's effeminate character *nachya* like a pansy. But I knew that that's not how I wanted to be. Even then I knew what I didn't want to be and that made me realize even more what I wanted to be.'

This made her even more determined to become a woman, at all costs.

'A *titli* (butterfly) is not beautiful in its cocoon. It becomes beautiful when it comes out. I was an insect who wanted to become a butterfly.'

Knowing that her family would not approve of her transition, Gauri ran away from home at the age of seventeen with Rs 60 in her pocket. The year was 1996.

Did she ever feel resentful or angry about being outcast merely for choosing to remain true to who she really is?

Don't open wounds that have just healed, she tells me. 'The truth is that people will keep a rapist and murderer in their house, but not a trans.'

'Of course, I am angry,' she continues. 'I get angry if someone stares directly at my breasts to check if I'm really a woman. Once I was at the airport and a man kept scratching himself while talking to me. It was disgusting. I asked him, "*Aapko khujali hai kya?* (Do you have a problem?)". I made him realize how obnoxious he was being, so that he never behaves like that with anyone else again.'

Did Gauri ever feel that it would have been easier to remain a boy? To not have to fight family and society to do what she wanted?

'No,' she says without a pause. 'I wasted my earlier years being a man. I felt like I didn't exist. Can you imagine how you would feel if you went out wearing a burkha and people assumed that you were a terrorist? Wouldn't it affect the way you feel? If changing your clothes can affect how people treat you, imagine what it is like to change your gender.'

So, Gauri came to Mumbai. She joined the transgender world, where she had a guru who supported her aspirations to become educated and a woman. As she struggled to settle into this new city, her father came to the rescue and bought her a house in Raheja Township in Malad.

'Settling me down was his way of trying to make up, not to me but to my mother,' Gauri laughs as she recalls. 'Apparently, my mother came to him in his dreams and she was crying. My father thought this was because he hadn't done anything for me.' For around two-three years her father transferred Rs 800 to Gauri's bank account every month. This helped meet her expenses, while she completed her education. Gauri then decided that she wanted to work. She joined the organization Humsafar Trust as an outreach worker.

While her life story could be lifted straight from a 1980s potboiler, Gauri gave it a 2080s twist. After she had saved some money, her first call of duty was to become a woman.

'I had to undergo many surgeries during my sex reassignment, but I didn't mind,' she says. 'I was so happy to have a penis out of me! It was such a relief. After my vaginoplasty, I knew that my struggle was complete. I was finally relaxed. I could finally love myself.'

'When I was a boy, I didn't care what clothes I wore. As a woman, I am so particular about what I wear because I have worked so hard to get this body. We (transgenders) love a woman's soul. We like dressing up, even if it is loud, because we are not afraid to claim the space that women occupy. In any temple we dress up our goddesses, so what's wrong if we humans do it?'

She pauses. I take that moment to observe that Gauri has had a smile on her face throughout our conversation. She makes her struggles seem so easy and simple.

She continues: 'In particular, I like voluptuous women in bindis and saris. That's why my purse has bindis in all colours and I always have a bindi on me. According to me, the bigger the bindi, the more powerful a woman is. After all, the bindi aligns with our chakras.' I notice that Gauri is wearing a long red bindi with a black outline. She continues: 'Earlier women put kumkum as it removes toxins from the body. The sindoor was worn with a middle parting to remove heat from the body. The nose ring was worn to decrease blood pressure. All these things had practical value. Nowadays, women reject traditional wear. I don't agree with these new notions. This is not pinjra tod.' Still, she does laugh at the outdated notion that a woman is given pearls to wear before marriage so that she doesn't stray with men, and a diamond after marriage so she becomes more sexual. 'Why is a woman's sexuality still tied to marriage?'

Four years after coming to Mumbai, in 2000, Gauri formed a community-based organization called 'Sakhi Char Chowghi' along with Ashok Row Kavi, one of India's most prominent LGBT rights activists, and two others. Her aim was to promote safe sex and provide counselling to transgenders and men who have sex with men (MSMs). Today, the organization has grown to a team of 150 workers.

'You may judge us or be scared of us, but life for transgenders is very tough,' she says. 'I worked with the NGO Shelter Don Bosco for three years, since I love working with street children, but they never recognized me. Eventually they threw me out because I was a transgender. If we get jobs, we won't be on the streets. If we get education, people will employ us. The truth is that we get neither.'

With these sentiments in mind, Gauri became a petitioner for the National Legal Services Authority (NALSA). It is partially due to her efforts that in 2013 the Supreme Court recognized transgenders as a third gender. Another milestone, yes, but five years later her community is still striving for basic civic rights.

'We are not English-speaking. We are vernacular. We are marginalized. It's easy to ignore us. That's why we are on the streets and at traffic signals.' She adds: 'Transgenders are shirked even by the LGBT community. It's sad that even gays and lesbians keep away from us.'

When will the third gender become a first priority?

'It will take centuries. Even in the Mahabharata, which was written in the eighth century, there was a transgender king called Shikhandi. India was so progressive then. Why have we become so regressive now?'

Through these long and arduous struggles, Gauri harboured one Panglossian desire: to be a mother. She recalls a conversation that she had with an aunt when she was barely ten years old. 'She asked me what I wanted to be when I grew up. Everyone thought I would say a police officer like my father. But I answered, "I want to be a mother." They all thought I was being facetious and told me that I could never be a mother. But I was determined that, somehow or the other, one day I would be.'

It was serendipity that then led her to this magnificent milestone.

'A pregnant sex worker used to come to our centre. She was HIV positive. I took a lot of care of her, giving her *nimbu ka aachar* (lemon pickle) and anything else that she craved for. Four-five years later I asked where she was and I was told that she was very sick. Then I heard that she had died and left behind her five-year-old daughter, Gayatri. This was 2001. I found out that Gayatri's grandmother had decided to sell Gayatri to a dealer in Sonagachi, Asia's largest red-light area in Kolkata. To save this small child from becoming a sex worker, I took her in for a few days. At that time I had no intention of adopting her. But, after a few days, when no one came to pick her up, I decided to make Gayatri my daughter. *Insaniyat ke naate,*' she explains. As a human being. 'I didn't adopt her with a piece of paper, I adopted her from the heart.'

Gayatri, whose name means hymn, entered like a song in Gauri's life.

Again, it wasn't easy. Gauri tells me that when she walks on the streets with Gayatri, some people look down upon them. 'I don't mind. Do you know that a *bichhoo* (scorpion) gives birth only once in its life? This is because its kids become hungry ten minutes after being born and eat the mother. A bichhoo sacrifices its own life in order to become a mother. I am like that bichhoo. Gayatri may grow up to not appreciate what I've done for her. She may even be embarrassed of me and disown me as her mother. But my job is to make her stand on her own two feet.'

The selflessness is amazing. The truth is that growing up without a mother or a mother's love, Gauri did not know what being a mother meant till she became one herself. Yet, she's willing to let herself be vulnerable and hurt. That's true love. That's a mother.

'I would not change this for anything. God made Gayatri for me. It is because of her that I became a mother, which is one of the truest manifestations of womanhood.

I feel so lucky to have her that I feel silly if I cry about anything else in my life.'

In the short time we spend together Gauri teaches me, a new mother, one true fact. That motherhood is not biological; it is emotional. She is a mother as much as I am. We share the same anticipation and the same anxiety for our daughters.

'Gayatri makes demands of me, like any daughter would,' Gauri adds. 'She tells me what to cook for her. She never keeps her things in place. She tells me, at the last minute, to do her school projects.' Gauri laughs. I find it remarkable that despite being deprived of the love a child receives, Gauri instinctively knows how a child needed to be loved.

'I never thought I would be this way, but I am a very protective mother. So, if Gayatri wants to get wet in the rain I will not stop her, but I will make sure that she is wearing a t-shirt and bra, and that no boys are watching her. I am all for women wearing what they want but I tell my own daughter to always wear a dupatta.' She laughs again.

Gauri adds that she is determined to give Gayatri a better life than the one she had. 'She can be anything she wants to be. I will always support her. She's not good at studies because she had a late start, so I insist that she must become a good human being and a sensitive person. She must take my name forward like Rahul Gandhi and Abhishek Bachchan do for their families. People should know me as her mother.'

Gauri takes a sip of tea and looks out at Mumbai's skyline that is growing dark with the setting sun. 'Being a parent has made me sensitive to why my father was angry with me. He must have been concerned. He knew that life treats transgenders cruelly, and he wanted to save me from that pain.' Gauri wipes the tear rolling down her cheek. 'Do you know that five years ago, I saw my father cross the road in front of me and I stopped the rickshaw? He was looking old and frail. I had only seen him as a strong police officer before. But I couldn't even call out to him. Imagine not being able to call out to your own father! I must be unlucky. Even today, after all my success, he does not let me reach out to him.'

But good things were in store for Gauri. An advertisement about Gauri and Gayatri's true-life story came out in April 2017. It went viral with millions of views. The mother–daughter story resonated with thousands of people from around the world. Gauri immediately shot to the limelight. Life came full circle. How has life changed since then?

'I enjoy the attention, and when people come to me to take selfies. But I also feel like I have become more responsible as people are looking up to me. The other day I was going to the international airport when an old transgender knocked on my window. I got out and touched his feet. I couldn't meet his eyes and tell him that I was travelling to America to represent his community, while he was out there begging on the street. Even after all my fights and struggles to improve things for my community, why are we on the streets? Why do people still look at us weirdly?'

I notice that everything about Gauri fills a void that she has seen in her own life. It amazes me that someone who has seen so little while growing up has so much to give. For her love doesn't restrict itself to humans—she's also actively involved in saving turtles and street dogs. She runs a shelter for young trans individuals who are turned away by their families, their grief echoing in the ghosts of memories past. She is also building a two-storeyed house called *Aaji Ka Ghar* (grandmother's house) for both abandoned children of sex workers and transgenders. She hopes to accommodate around eighty children who can be given the right education, food and care so that they can have a loving childhood.

'The idea for *Aaji Ka Ghar* came one day when I had gone to the red-light area of Kamathipura. There I met two Bangladeshi girls who went to get me paan. As I waited for them, I sat in front of a curtain. I heard some noises behind me. I drew the curtain and saw a baby girl playing with her mother's dupatta, while an old man was on top of her mother. I felt terrible. But what choice did the mother have? She was obviously making money for her own daughter. This hit me. I'm ok if a woman is sleeping with ten men, but not out of force. That is *not* ok. That's when I decided to help these girls.'

Aaji Ka Ghar will be India's first transgender house run by transgenders. 'It's my dream,' Gauri says. 'To build this house I am using my own land. I was also working as a judge for a show on TV9 that helped us raise more funds for the house.'

To serve oneself before others, and serve others before oneself, it's been a long journey for Gauri. Shunned. Ostracized. Judged. Sidelined. It is remarkable how she hasn't succumbed to these travesties, how she's chosen not to make this the matrix in which she lives her life. How has she come out positive?

'Some pickles become sweet with time, while others become sour. I have no reason to be negative,' she says. This is remarkable. 'Think about it. If I were "normal", I wouldn't be where I am. I know that God sent me here to be a watchman in our society, a gardener in our garden. Therefore, I do my karma. I am answerable to god, not humans.'

I know what she's saying. The same boiling water that softens the potato hardens the egg. It's about what you're made of and not your circumstances.

'I am still fighting for things like my right to adoption,' she adds. 'I am fighting for my child's right to inherit my property after my death so that she can have a secure life. I'm fighting for every Indian and for every mother.'

Why prolong her struggles? Why not rest on her laurels?

'Do you accept yourself as a second gender?' she asks me. Never, I say. 'Then don't accept me as a third gender.' Point noted. 'Gender is not in your genitals, it's in your mind,' she adds. 'This is what I will continue fighting for.'

As must we all.

We decide to take a break and I offer her some snacks. I am vegetarian, she tells me. She goes on to add that she believes in Sai Baba of Shirdi and Shankaracharya, due to which she fasts every Thursday and Sunday, respectively. A breath later she tells me, 'Even though I'm spiritual, I am very flirty. I love dirty talk. If I see a man, I mentally undress him.' I look at her and smile. She is spiritual and sexual. During the course of this conversation, she has addressed herself as both a scorpion and a butterfly. While she is brash, I find in her a rare stillness. How does she possess such dualities?

'We are all two things. I can be as cold as an air-conditioner and as hot as a geyser. It depends on the situation. Look at Saraswati and Kali, they are so different but we treat them both as our goddesses.'

This leads me to my next question. I ask her what feminism means to her.

'Your shadow is with you but you can't catch it. It is with you in the sun and not in the shade. Feminism is like that. It is with you but you can't describe it. But if I had to define it, I would say feminism is: Respect gender equality for all. Embrace your own sexuality. Treat everyone with love.'

I don't need Gauri to admit that she's a feminist. Her actions speak loud enough. Still—

'To me, being myself is being a feminist. I am original, authentic, loud and not scared of anything. I am not ashamed of my body or my tone of voice. I don't tolerate nonsense. Even most feminists will not possess my bindaas-ness (carefree attitude). If a man is not good in bed, I will tell him. Most feminists will not be able to do that.' She laughs again.

Could the seventeen-year-old Gauri have imagined that within twenty years she would be all these things—woman, mother, activist and celebrity? No, she admits wistfully. What else is she imagining herself to be, the what next that seems impossible?

'I don't know. I know that now people look up to me as a community leader. I know that I owe them a responsibility. I can't drink and drive. I can't beg on the streets. I have to work more. I have to be clear and focused. I feel like my journey has just started.'

I press her.

'Maybe the Prime Minister of India!' she says.

Now that would make for some good news.

She is a devoted mother who didn't have a mother. She is a kind activist who didn't receive kindness. She is a proud trans who was shamed for her identity. There is a term in Sanskrit: *Vasudhaiva Kutumbakam*. It means bringing the world together like a family. And Gauri is doing this marvellously, one gender at a time.